Retro Happy Hour

Retro

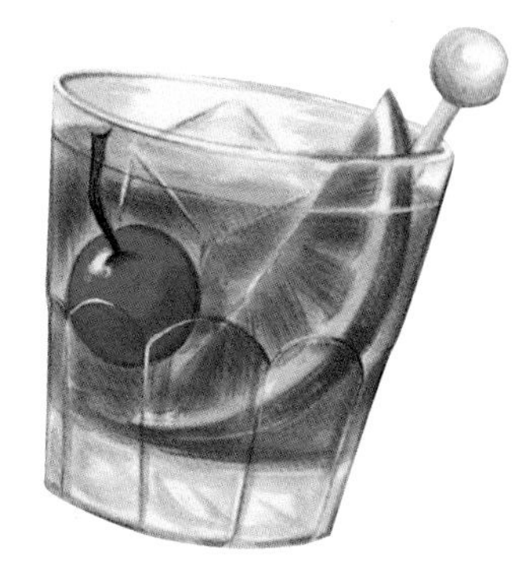

Happy Hour

Drinks and Eats With a '50s Beat

PORTLAND, OREGON

Library of Congress Cataloging-in-Publication Data
Everett, Linda, 1946-
Retro happy hour : drinks and eats with a '50s beat / by Linda Everett.
p. cm.
Includes Index.
ISBN 1-888054-76-X
1. Cocktail parties. 2. Appetizers. 3. Beverages. I. Title.
TX731 .E94 2003
642'.4--dc21
2002015240

Design: Evan Holt
Editor: Sue Mann
Vintage Cocktail items courtesy of Ralph Griggs.

Printed in Singapore
First American edition
9 8 7 6 5 4 3 2 1

Collectors Press books are available at special discounts for bulk purchases, premiums, and promotions. Special editions, including personalized inserts or covers, and corporate logos, can be printed in quantity for special purposes. For further information contact: Special Sales, Collectors Press, Inc., P.O. Box 230986, Portland, OR 97281. Toll-free: 1-800-423-1848

For a free catalog write:
Collectors Press, Inc.
P.O. Box 230986, Portland, OR 97281
Toll-free: 1-800-423-1848
Or visit our website at: www.collectorspress.com

Contents

Introduction

JUMP INTO THE era of the 1950s and you'll find the consummate host and hostess mingling among their guests during the perfect party. The Missus is dolled up in her heels, pearls, and cocktail dress, offering a brightly colored Fiestaware platter of appetizers. Hubby's duty is to oversee the bar in his Brooks Brothers suit and silk tie adorned with palm trees. The concept was to start out the evening with a warm-up happy hour: tempt, but not quench, the appetite for that gourmet meal. Finish out the picture with creative decorations, perhaps some entertainment, and friends would be talking about the bash for months.

The 1950's housewife worried about what to serve and whether the guests would enjoy her efforts. The hostess of today may not drag out her mother's pearls, but she still hopes to see the party start out right, with appetizers and drinks invigorating the conversation and putting everyone at ease.

Every hostess wants everything to be just perfect for the occasion. But good parties don't just happen — it takes work, planning, some thought, and maybe a crumb of creativity. It doesn't even have to zero out your bank account (unless you want it to). Follow the hints, rules, recipes, and suggestions in this book and your party will be a sure-fire success!

Let's Celebrate!

Chapter 1

Theme! Theme! Theme!

SO! YOU'VE DECIDED to throw a party! Perhaps beer and a take-out pizza will fulfill your notion of the perfect bash. However, to celebrate a special occasion and make it memorable to all who partake, planning is the key. And first on the agenda is what type of party.

Consider a theme and run with it. The motif could be in conjunction with a holiday, the Big Game, or perhaps the Country Music Awards, or Oscars. Coming up with a theme for any of these can be a snap, or you could use your creativity and go a little wild. How about a Christmas picnic or barbecue? A royal bash for your hubby? A down-home Smoky Mountain hoedown for your best friend's retirement fete?

You get the idea.

Suggestions for Your Party Theme

Putting together a celebration for that big moment in someone's life — a promotion, retirement, once-in-a-lifetime trip, graduation, birthday, or wedding — should also be a challenge to your imagination. Going with what the guest of honor likes or enjoys is fine, but also consider browsing through thrift stores, dollar stores, and other discount outlets for weird, fun, unusual, or inspired party ideas. For example: you might come across a monumentally ugly, huge old chair and decide to use it as a throne for the guest of honor. Or, try rental stores for something like a group of elegant slinky mannequins you can dress as celebrities, royalty, funky '60s flower children, or high-class models in wild fashions you've designed. The point is to use your imagination!

If you need a little boost you might check out *Chase's Annual Events* by William and Mary Chase. This book

"I Hear You're Having a Party"

lists every known and barely known holiday, celebration, and event for practically each day of the year. Your local library should have a copy.

Here are two more theme ideas:

Ski party: This would be even more fun in the summer! Think ahead at those after-Christmas sales and pick up sheets of fake snow and cans of spray snow. Check out thrift and second-hand stores for old skis, ski poles, ski boots, grog mugs, and more.

Income Tax party: Copy blank income tax forms for invitations. Set the table with plain paper, or even newspaper, and the cheapest paper plates and plastic wear. Serve Hobo Stew and crackers. Decorate with black crepe paper and bouquets of dead flowers.

Ten Tips for the Absolute Perfect Party

1. Theme: See "Suggestions for Your Party Theme." This includes your food, decorations, and ambiance.
2. Guests: See "The Guest List." How many will you invite?
3. Food: First decide what your budget will allow. Consider party-pooling: going together with friends to throw the bash and share the cost of food, decorations, work, etc. Then make a complete and careful shopping list after checking your pantry.
4. Help: Even if you've thrown parties, think about how much time you spent enjoying your guests. Maybe you should hire some help -- consider a high school or college student to assist with putting it all together, serving, and the dreaded cleaning up. If you do, write down all your instructions in detail. Another alternative is to spend the money for a professional caterer.
5. Fun: Lights! Music! Games!
6. Invitations: See "Making Your Own Cool/Fun/Classy Invitations."
7. Clean the house: Don't leave this until the last moment. If need be, hire some help, or at least start several days before the big bash.
8. Set up the party room: If you're fortunate enough to have a family room, basement, patio, sizable living room, or even a nice garage, try to get it ready and decorated a day or two before the party.
9. Buy the food and beverages: Do this a few days before if you can.
10. Plan! Plan! Plan!: Make lists, get as much as possible done ahead of time, relax, and enjoy!

The Guest List

How many people will you invite? The temptation is to invite all your friends and their third cousins. Consider how much space you have and be reasonable.

If it's a sit-down dinner, you will need to plan the seating. You probably know these people well enough so you won't put the organic gardener next to the chemical engineer. Try placing new people next to not-so-new to help them mix in. You might also alternate men and women or the get-together could turn into a guy party/girl party.

Making Your Own Cool/Fun/Classy Invitations

- If this is a formal occasion, send out invitations three to four weeks in advance. If it's a casual affair, two weeks is fine.
- Include the following information:
  - Reason for the party
  - Date and day of the week
  - Time (start and end)
  - Place (include a map if needed)
  - Any necessary details (bring your swimsuit)
  - Dress code (black tie optional, grubbies, Hawaiian, ski attire, Halloween, costume ball, or casual.
- Be sure to include an R.S.V.P.
- Remember to double check your guest list to make sure you haven't left anyone out.

Here are a few novel ideas for invitations. Use your imagination and the same suggestions for theme decorations (see page 10).

Valentine (or something romantic) Party

Have a professional print invitations that look like actual wedding invitations. Make color copies of borrowed snapshots of the couple. Use for the front of your invitations.

- Buy postcards of the famous Grant Wood painting, *American Gothic,* and use for the front of the invitations.
- Dig through your family documents and if possible color copy and reduce in size old marriage certificates. Print party information on reverse side (either by hand, calligraphy if you can, or on your computer) and fold into correct size for envelope.
- Copy an old marriage certificate (see above), blank out information, and fill in with party details.
- Cut out doves from heavy white paper, punch a hole in each, and tie together with a piece of beautiful thin white ribbon. Mail in envelope with a little sparkling confetti in the bottom.

- Cut out hearts from nice art paper; punch hole in each, and follow directions for doves. This time use the valentine mixture of confetti.
- Track down old magazines from the year the honored couple were married. Color copy photos or ads of wedding couples.
- Cut out photos of famous lovers and make color copies for the invitations. Drop a sprinkle of confetti hearts into the envelopes.

Christmas Party

The following four invitations need to be hand delivered. They might also be more appropriate for a small get-together.

- Buy 6-inch candy canes and on each attach a cutout star, tree, or angel with a nice ribbon. Print or use calligraphy to put the party information on the back.
- Buy small (6-inch) craft Christmas trees. Plant in tiny clay pots. Decorate and either attach a cutout as mentioned above or paint information on the pot with puffypaint.*
- Bake your invitations. Make a dough of 4 cups flour, 1 cup salt, and 1¾ cups water. Roll out and cut with Christmas-theme cookie cutters. Make a hole at the top of each and bake on foil at 250 degrees 2 to 3 hours. Write party details on the back with colored felt-tipped pen, puffy paint*, or acrylic paints.
- Buy small, inexpensive flat ornaments and on each attach a cut-out star with information written on it in colorful ink.
- Cut out wreaths and decorate. Either attach to the fronts of your blank invitations or write party information around them. Mail.
- Make color copies of vintage or antique Christmas scenes and either fold as the invitation or use for the front. A favorite Christmas poem is also another nice idea.

New Year's Eve

- If your party is a costume ball, buy inexpensive paper masks, write party information on the back, and mail.
- Buy inexpensive party hats, write party information on the back, and mail.
- Buy miniature champagne glasses. Write party details with gold or silver ink on the glasses. Tie curly ribbon around the stems and glue some bright confetti inside. Mail in small boxes or hand deliver.
- Write information on deflated New Year's Eve balloons. Put in envelopes with some of that colorful confetti.

Miscellaneous Invitation Ideas

- Seed packets, travel brochures, a silk flower, a paper party hat, copy of an award or certificate, a square of material (like a Hawaiian print for that luau), a small fancy napkin, or...

*Puffy Paint: Mix equal parts of flour, salt, and water. Add food coloring until desired color is acheived. Put in a squeeze bottle and pipe out letters. Let dry. Mixture will harden into puffy letters.

Fun! Fun! Fun!

Let the Music Begin!!

- Do you have a good stereo system or can you borrow one from a trusting friend? Check through your CDs and figure out if you need to borrow some of those as well.
- Designate someone to be in charge of the tunes. Remember: the music is part of that all-critical theme and should fit in. You might set up a play list.
- If your theme is a '50's,'60s, or '70s dance party, you might need to locate an older stereo that plays records. Check out thrift and second-hand stores; quite often you can find a perfectly good record player for a pittance, especially because records are now passe'. Records are also a steal at places like Goodwill and Salvation Army — usually 50 cents to a dollar.
- Check out stores that deal in used CDs and records for music, especially party mixes and compilations of the oldies. Browse through the oddball, weird, and fun categories, too, for something different and also for sound effects.

- ✢ "Hey! I'm with the band!" If a friend of a friend of your second cousin doesn't know of a decent local band, look through your yellow pages and newspaper entertainment section. Make sure the band comes highly recommended; better yet, listen to it in person or at least on tape. (Nothing's worse than lousy music. It could squelch the whole party.)
- ✢ Depending upon the type or theme of the party, a single musician, such as a classical guitarist, might be a wonderful touch.

Games: There are heaps of books on party games available in second-hand bookstores, regular bookstores, and, of course, the library. Try to avoid getting stuck in the rut of old boring clichés like pin-the-tail-on-the-donkey.

That's What I Call Entertainment!: If your budget can handle it, consider hiring professional entertainment other than a band: a magician, juggler, fortune-teller, comedian, clown, or Santa. Be creative!

The Eats

Chapter 2

IF YOU'RE AN old hand at sit-down dinners with fancy food you spent days preparing — hooray for you! Otherwise, start with simple, easy-to-eat finger foods. The next step up might be a Baked-Tater party (see page 58), barbecue, dessert party, salad bar party, or make-your-own pizza. Some food rules to remember:

- Try the recipes ahead of time!
- Get a system down for making numerous items such as the appetizers. If you can bribe the kids, get an assembly line going.
- If you're making an appetizer or snack that freezes well, make a double or even larger batch and freeze some for a future bash.
- Make sure you have all your ingredients beforehand so there are no last-minute frantic runs to the supermarket.
- A few days before the party make sure you have all the utensils, pots, pans, and cooking appliances needed and ready to use.
- Double-check the ingredients you need for beverages.

A Good Motto: Be Prepared!

If you entertain more than occasionally (more than the required turkey toss at Thank-you-very-much time), this list is for you! Try to keep at least a few of these items on hand.

Cheese: Especially something nice. The deli department of most markets is now a cheese-lover's heaven.

Cheese spreads: Yes, these can be mundane, but there are some great combinations in your deli department or specialty store. In a pinch any of these can be a boon. If you can afford to pick up a jar or two of the more elegant varieties — perfect!

Canned tuna: Wait! Not the cheap stuff! The basic should be at least a premium albacore. Move on from there to smoked, garlic, and other treats.

Canned salmon: The same goes for salmon: great specialty flavors as well as the main ingredient for several superb dips and appetizers.

Smoked salmon: It's spendy but a little goes a long way. The flavor is divine.

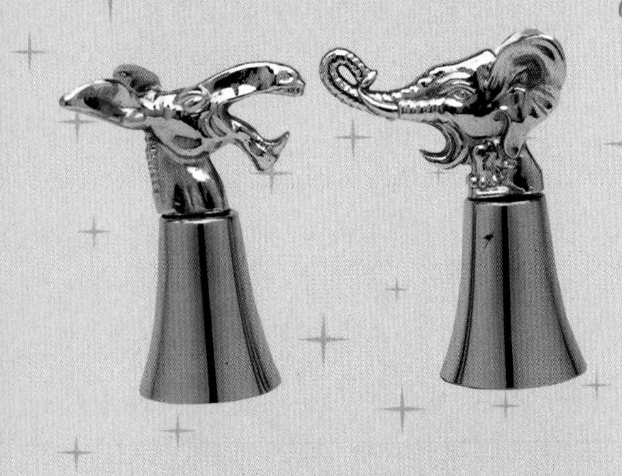

Canned meats: Deviled ham, chicken (both whole canned and the spreads), liverwurst, corned beef, and more.

Those little sausages everyone serves at Superbowl parties: These minifranks can be smoked or plain, good or not so good. Check out the dipping sauces for a change from the ol' barbecue.

Salted nuts: Check out the different flavors. The canned ones will keep for quite awhile, but keep track of the expiration date! Look over the recipes for yummy variations like Tokyo Knockouts on page 25.

Pickles: The varieties seem to grow by the week, but think about trying some of the quick recipes for homemade, like Quick Sweet/Dill Pickles on page 20.

Olives: A good standby, but don't be lazy and simply dump out a can in a bowl and plunk it on the coffee table. Check out the ideas on page 20.

Popcorn: Wow! I'm a popcorn fanatic! Try the recipes starting on page 28.

Crackers: Use your imagination. Try a discount or canned food store for imported and other unusual varieties.
Check out the recipes for your own homemade crackers on page 47.

Chips: Like popcorn and crackers, grocery shelves are packed with all sorts of flavors. Don't forget the wide variety of tortilla chips, too! Try something new with the dips on page 21.

Hurry-up Eats!

This segment contains a time-friendly array of party-proven recipes.

- Stuff large- to jumbo-size black olives with Roquefort cheese. Stand olives on end in a fun container.
- Spread squares of dried chipped beef with softened cream cheese (sprinkle on a few chives if you like). Roll, wrap in foil, and chill. When ready to serve remove foil remove foil and slice in 1-inch sections.

Quick Sweet/Dill Pickles

1 pound 3-inch pickling cukes
1 large or two small sweet onions (like Walla Wallas, Vidalia, or Maui)
4 tsps salt
3 tblsps water
¾ cup white sugar
½ cup apple cider vinegar
1 tsp dried or 3 heads of fresh dill weed (or to taste)

1. In your food processor run the cukes and onions until thinly sliced.

2. In a large glass or similar nonaluminum bowl, mix the cuke mixture with salt and water and let sit about 2 hours in the refrigerator.

3. Drain cuke mixture but don't rinse. Mix in sugar, vinegar, and dill. Let stand until sugar dissolves; stir occasionally. When liquid rises and covers cuke mixture (about an hour), pack in freezer containers leaving 1 inch of space at the top, label, and freeze.

4. To serve: defrost either in refrigerator or at room temperature.

Last-Second Dips

Serve any of the following as a quick dip with crackers, chips, melba toast, or crusty sourdough chunks.

In your blender or food processor zap together:

- 1 can drained albacore tuna, 1 stick softened butter (has to be the real stuff), a dash of garlic powder, and ½ tsp parsley (fresh or dried).
- 1 3-oz. package softened cream cheese with 4 stuffed green olives, 10 blanched almonds, and 1 tblsp mayonnaise.
- 1 3-oz. package softened cream cheese with ¼ cup canned drained pineapple and a dash of horseradish.
- 1 3-oz. package softened cream cheese with 1 2 ¼-oz. can deviled ham, ½ tsp lemon juice, and ½ tsp horseradish.
- 1 3-oz. package softened cream cheese with 3 tblsps blue cheese and 1 2 ¼-oz. can deviled ham.
- 1 stick butter with 1 cup finely chopped canned, drained shrimp. Add 1 tblsp lemon juice, 1 tsp prepared mustard, 1 tsp Worcestershire sauce, ½ tsp salt, dash of coarsely ground black pepper.
- 1 3-oz. package softened cream cheese with 1 can drained sardines, 1 tsp. grated onion, dash each of horseradish, salt, coarsely ground black pepper, and paprika.

Quick Mini-Kabobs

For skewers use those colorful cocktail toothpicks. You may want to poke a hole in the food with a metal skewer beforehand. Here are some combinations.

Cold:

- Swiss cheese and salami chunks
- Cooked chicken chunks and chunks of jicama
- Ham and sharp cheddar cheese chunks
- Stuffed olives and Monterey Jack cheese (or other mild-flavored cheese)
- Ham and fresh pineapple chunks (canned will work)
- Salami chunks and chunks of apple
- Shrimp and mandarin orange slices
- Ripe olives and little smoky franks
- Ham and yellow or red pepper

Hot:

Wrap a slice of bacon around any of the following and skewer with a toothpick. Broil until bacon is crisp, turning once or twice.

- Pineapple chunks (fresh or canned)
- Shelled and deveined shrimp
- Those famous little franks, smoke-flavored or plain
- Raw scallops
- Small oysters, cooked or raw
- 1-inch chunks of a firm fish, such as halibut or lingcod, cooked
- Chunks of canned pears or peaches
- Chunks of luncheon meat
- Small mushrooms
- Chicken livers, cooked

Purple Heaven!

Drain a can of beets and rinse; place in a quart jar with ½ cup apple cider vinegar, ¼ cup good oil (I like extra virgin olive oil), 4 tblsps brown sugar, and a dash each of salt and coarsely ground black pepper. Put on lid and store in refrigerator at least 2 days, turning jar and shaking gently several times.

Elfin Mushrooms

Drain 3 small cans of button mushrooms and dump into a pint jar. Pour in ½ cup apple cider vinegar, ¼ cup oil, dash each of salt and coarsely ground black pepper, ½ tsp Worcestershire sauce, and ¼ tsp dry mustard. Store in refrigerator 2 days before serving, turning frequently.

Miracle Lake Mushrooms

½ cup water
3 pounds fresh small mushrooms, washed and drained
3-4 tblsps olive oil
1 tsp dried parsley (or 2 tsps fresh, finely chopped)
1 ½ cups bread crumbs (for a variety try the Italian seasoned kind)
6 tblsps grated Parmesan cheese (or try sharp Cheddar or another favorite)
½ tsp salt
½ tsp coarsely ground black pepper

1. Preheat oven to 350 degrees.
2. Grease a shallow baking pan. Pour water in the bottom.
3. Pop the stems out of mushrooms (save for soup, other dip, or spread). Arrange mushrooms bottom side up in baking pan, sprinkle with oil.
4. In a small bowl mix parsley, crumbs, cheese, salt, and pepper.
5. Sprinkle mixture over mushrooms and bake 45 minutes. Top should be lightly browned.

Serves 15

Tokyo Knockouts

1. Preheat oven to 325 degrees.

2. Spread 2 cups of your favorite nuts on a large ungreased baking sheet. Roast in oven 5 to 10 minutes or until lightly browned.

3. In a small skillet melt 2 tblsps butter or margarine and stir in 1 tblsp soy sauce, ½ tsp ground ginger, dash of garlic salt, and 1 tsp lemon juice.

4. Remove from heat and brush butter mixture over toasted nuts. Roast 5 minutes more until golden brown.

Makes 2 cups

Southern Belle Hot Pecans

1. Preheat oven to 350 degrees.

2. Spread 2 cups pecan halves over large baking sheet and roast 7 minutes to heat through.

3. In a small bowl combine 3 tblsps melted butter, 1 tsp chili powder, dash of cayenne pepper, 1 garlic clove crushed (or 1 tsp minced garlic from a jar), ¼ tsp salt, and dash of ground coriander.

4. Remove pecans from oven and brush with butter mixture. Roast 5 minutes more.

Makes 2 cups

Smoky Mountain Almond Nibblers

1. Preheat oven to 350 degrees.

2. Spread 2 cups whole blanched almonds on large baking sheet and roast 8 to 10 minutes until light golden brown.

3. In a small bowl combine 2 tblsps melted butter, dash of seasoned salt, ½ tsp liquid smoke seasoning, and dash of garlic salt.

4. Remove almonds from oven and brush generously with butter mixture.

5. Return to oven and bake 5 minutes more.

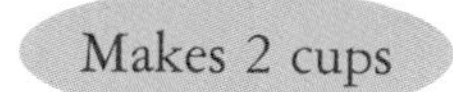
Makes 2 cups

Aunt Lucy's Famous Walnuts

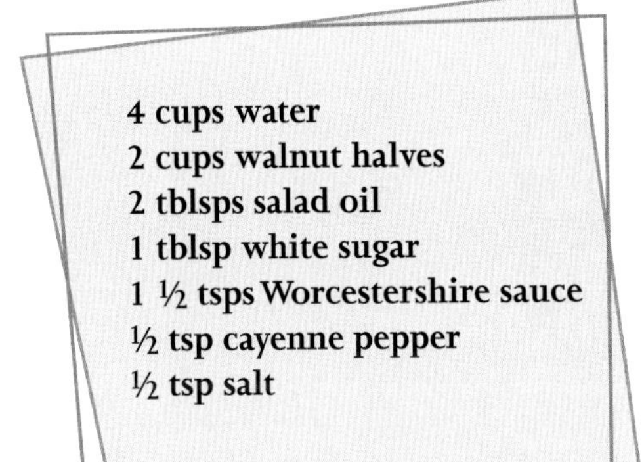
4 cups water
2 cups walnut halves
2 tblsps salad oil
1 tblsp white sugar
1 ½ tsps Worcestershire sauce
½ tsp cayenne pepper
½ tsp salt

1. In a large saucepan heat water to boiling over high; add walnuts and reheat to boiling. Boil 1 minute.

2. Rinse walnuts under hot running water; drain and pat dry with paper towels.

3. Thoroughly wash saucepan and pat dry to eliminate walnut oils. In the same saucepan heat oil, add walnuts, sugar, Worcestershire sauce, pepper, and salt.

4. Cook, stirring constantly about 5 to 7 minutes or until lightly browned.

5. Remove walnuts with a slotted spoon to paper towels; drain and cool. Store in tightly covered container. Use within 2 weeks.

Makes 2 cups

Popcorn! Ah! Popcorn!

Indiana Anna's Basic Popcorn Balls

5 quarts freshly popped corn
4 cups white sugar
2 tsps salt
1 cup water
2 tblsps butter (sorry, margarine doesn't get it)
¼ tsp cream of tartar
butter for hands

1. Pour popcorn into a large bowl.
2. In a large saucepan over medium heat stir together sugar, salt, water, butter, and cream of tartar. Stir constantly until mixture reaches firm ball candy stage (245 degrees on candy thermometer. Another method of testing is to dip a spoon in the mixture and let it drip. Mixture should sheet as it drips).
3. Pour syrup over popcorn and stir gently with a large spoon to coat popcorn well.
4. Lightly butter hands and shape popcorn into 3-inch balls.
5. Cool on greased cookie sheets or waxed paper.

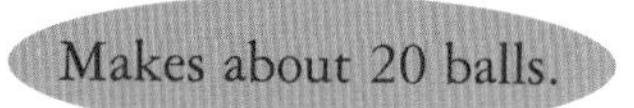

Gottahaveit!

5 cups freshly popped corn
1 cup white sugar
⅓ cup light corn syrup
½ cup water
3 tblsps butter or margarine
(not the diet kind!)
3 squares unsweetened chocolate, melted
butter for hands

1. Pour popcorn into a large bowl.

2. In a medium saucepan add sugar, corn syrup, water, butter, and chocolate, stir together, and bring to the hard ball (245 degrees) candy stage. (See Indiana Anna's Basic Popcorn Balls, p.28, for testing information.)

3. Pour slowly over popcorn and mix well but quickly to coat.

4. Butter your hands and shape popcorn into 3-inch balls. Cool on greased cookie sheets or waxed paper.

Makes about 20 balls

White Rabbit

5 cups freshly popped corn
1 tsp salt
¼ cup butter
½ lb.marshmallows
butter for hands

1. Pour hot popcorn into a large bowl; sprinkle with salt.

2. In a small skillet or saucepan melt butter over low heat.

3. With kitchen scissors cut marshmallows into chunks (about quarters) and stir into butter until well blended.

4. Pour over popcorn and mix well. Butter hands and form popcorninto 3-inch balls.

5. Cool on greased cookie sheets or waxed paper.

Makes about 20 balls

Front Porch Nibblin' Corn

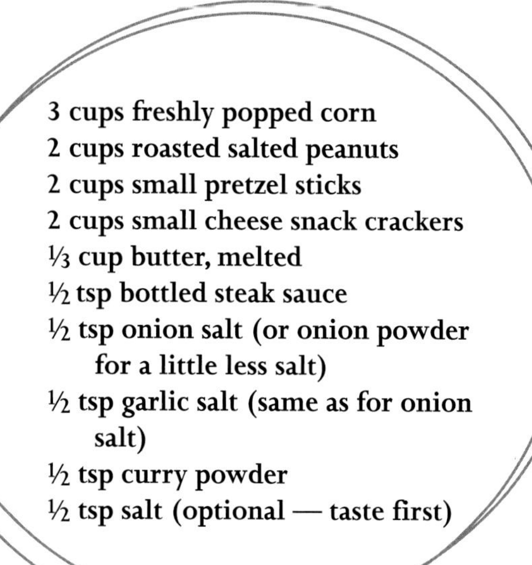

- 3 cups freshly popped corn
- 2 cups roasted salted peanuts
- 2 cups small pretzel sticks
- 2 cups small cheese snack crackers
- ⅓ cup butter, melted
- ½ tsp bottled steak sauce
- ½ tsp onion salt (or onion powder for a little less salt)
- ½ tsp garlic salt (same as for onion salt)
- ½ tsp curry powder
- ½ tsp salt (optional — taste first)

1. In a large roasting pan combine popped corn, peanuts, pretzels, and crackers.

2. In a small bowl mix butter, steak sauce, onion salt, garlic salt, curry powder, and optional salt.

3. Pour this coating mixture over ingredients in roasting pan and toss well.

4. Heat oven to 250 degrees and bake about 1 hour, stirring every 15 minutes.

5. Cool (although I prefer it warm). Store in airtight container. Can be stored in freezer several months so you can make a big batch ahead.

State Fair Caramel Corn

5 cups popped corn
1 cup butter or margarine (2 sticks)
½ cup light corn syrup
2 cups brown sugar
1 tsp salt
½ tsp baking soda

1. Spread popcorn in a large shallow baking pan and keep in a slow (250 degrees) oven to keep warm and crispy.

2. In a heavy saucepan combine butter, corn syrup, brown sugar, and salt. Cook over medium heat, stirring until sugar is dissolved. Bring to a gentle boil and continue to boil until syrup reaches the firm ball (245 degrees) candy stage (see Indiana Anna's Basic Popcorn Balls, p.28, for testing information). Continue cooking about 5 minutes more.

3. Remove syrup from heat and stir in baking soda. Mixture will foam.

4. Take popcorn from oven and dribble syrup over it in a fine stream. Mix well.

5. Return to oven another 45 to 50 minutes, stirring every 15 minutes. Cool and serve or store in an airtight container.

Hippie Jane's Honeyed Delight

5 cups popped corn
1 cup brown sugar, firmly packed
½ cup wild honey
½ cup water
¼ cup butter (Jane says home churned, but...)
butter for hands

1. Pour popcorn into a metal dishpan (okay, a large popcorn bowl will do) and keep in a warm oven.

2. In a heavy saucepan combine brown sugar, honey, and water. Heat slowly, stirring often, until sugar is dissolved.

3. Continue cooking until firm ball (245 degrees) candy stage (see Indiana Anna's Basic Popcorn Balls, p. 28, for testing information).

4. Remove from heat and stir in butter only enough to mix in. Slowly dribble syrup over warm popcorn and mix thoroughly.

5. Butter hands lightly and form popcorn into 3-inch balls. Cool on greased cookie sheets or waxed paper.

Makes about 20 balls

Snappy Popcorn Variations

1. Cheese: Add ½ cup dry grated sharp cheese to ¼ cup melted butter. Pour over freshly popped corn; salt to taste. Toss lightly and serve while warm.

2. Nutty: To ¼ cup melted butter add a heaping tablespoon of peanut butter (creamy or crunchy). Pour over hot popcorn and toss.

3. Herb: To ¼ cup melted butter add your favorite herbs: ½ tsp garlic powder, basil, thyme, maybe oregano? How about a little chili powder with cumin? Pour over popcorn and toss.

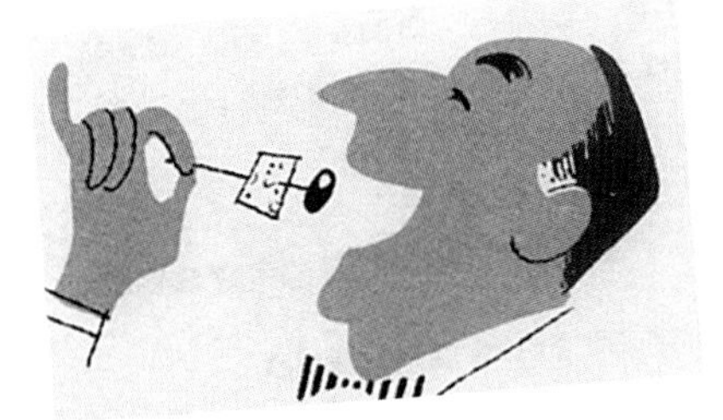

This sauce wears a wide variety of hats. You can serve it with meats, chicken, and other grilled goodies. But here it dips in all its glory on toasted chunks of sourdough or gooped on crisp, freshly baked pizza dough that's been primed with olive oil...yum!

Gotcha Sauce!

1 tblsp butter (yeah, the cow kind)
1 medium sweet onion, peeled and sliced very thin
1 large clove of garlic, peeled and minced (about 1 ½ tsps)
1 ½ pounds ripe tomatoes, cubed
¼ cup horseradish
½ tsp salt
dash of cayenne pepper (more if you like)
½ tsp fresh thyme (or ¼ tsp dried)

1. In a large skillet melt butter over medium heat and dump in onion. Keep stirring until onion begins to soften. Add garlic and continue cooking until onion is translucent.

2. Add tomatoes and horseradish. Continue cooking over medium-low heat, stirring occasionally, until tomatoes are tender, about 20 minutes.

3. Add salt, cayenne, and thyme. Serve either as is (chunky) or zap in your blender or food processor until well mixed but still a bit coarse.

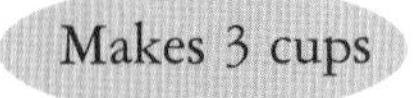
Makes 3 cups

Dockside Seafood Sauce

1. In a medium saucepan melt butter over low heat, whisk in flour, and slowly pour in milk. Stir until thickened.

2. Add shrimp, scallops, mushrooms, parsley, tarragon, nutmeg, salt, and pepper.

3. Serve with thin toasted bread triangles, chunks of sourdough, or any good dippin' bread or crackers.

3 tblsps butter
2 tblsps flour
1 cup milk, scalded
1/2 pound shrimp, chopped
1/2 pound scallops
1/2 cup mushrooms, sliced
1/2 cup parsley, chopped
1 tsp tarragon
dash nutmeg
salt and pepper to taste

Makes 3 cups

Burnin' Luv Crab Dip

1 6-oz. can crabmeat or 1 6-oz. package frozen crabmeat, thawed
1 3-oz. package cream cheese, at room temperature
1/2 cup dairy sour cream
1/2 tsp prepared horseradish (optional)
1 tblsp fresh lemon juice
1 tblsp minced pimiento
2 tblsps minced sweet onion (must be mild!)
1 French baguette or other small-diameter sourdough, sliced, or your favorite crackers or chips

1. Drain and flake canned or thawed crabmeat; set aside.

2. In a medium saucepan combine cream cheese, sour cream, horseradish, and lemon juice. Stir well.

3. Add pimiento, onion, and crabmeat. Heat over low, stirring constantly until bubbly.

4. Keep warm in a fondue or other pot over a candle.

5. Serve with crusty bread (I prefer toasted) or other dippers. Don't leave out leftovers more than an hour or so.

Makes 2 cups

Rio Grande Dip

2 slices lean bacon
1 small sweet onion, finely chopped
3 medium ripe tomatoes, peeled, seeded, chopped (or equivalent of canned)
1 clove garlic, finely chopped
½ cup celery, finely chopped
1 4-oz. can green chilies, chopped, drained
¼ tsp salt
2 cups Monterey Jack cheese, grated
Tortilla chips or crusty sourdough bread

1. In a medium skillet cook bacon until crisp; drain on paper towels.

2. Save about 1 tblsp of fat. Add onion, tomatoes (if using fresh), garlic, and celery and cook over medium heat, stirring often, until tender but not browned. Add canned tomatoes, if using, at this time.

3. Stir in salt. Reduce heat to low and gently stir in cheese, being careful not to boil.

4. Serve in a fondue pot or over some sort of very low heat.

5. Serve with a colorful variety of tortilla chips, dipping-style Fritos or potato chips, or chunks of crusty sourdough bread.

Makes 4 cups

Rojo Red's Famous Dippin' Stuff

1. In a small bowl combine mayonnaise, vinegar, chili sauce, curry powder, garlic powder, pepper, salt, and thyme.

2. Cover and refrigerate at least 1 hour; overnight is better. Garnish with parsley.

3. Serve with an assortment of fresh vegetables such as celery sticks, cherry tomatoes, baby carrots, cauliflowerets, broccoli heads, zucchini sticks, jicama sticks, green/red/yellow pepper strips, or green onions.

1 cup mayonnaise
2 tsps tarragon vinegar
1 tblsp chili sauce (if you have a favorite, go for it)
½ tsp curry powder
dash of garlic powder
½ tsp coarsely ground pepper
½ tsp salt
dash of dried thyme leaves, crumbled
½ tsp fresh parsley, finely chopped

Makes 1 cup

Portland's Mostest Bestest Dip

1. Preheat oven to 400 degrees.

2. Chop artichoke hearts and drain again. In a medium bowl combine artichoke hearts, crabmeat, mayonnaise, Parmesan cheese, garlic powder, and lemon juice.

3. Spread in a 1-quart baking dish and bake 15 to 20 minutes or until bubbly.

4. Serve hot with chunks of sourdough, toasted slices of baguette, or crackers.

Makes 4 cups

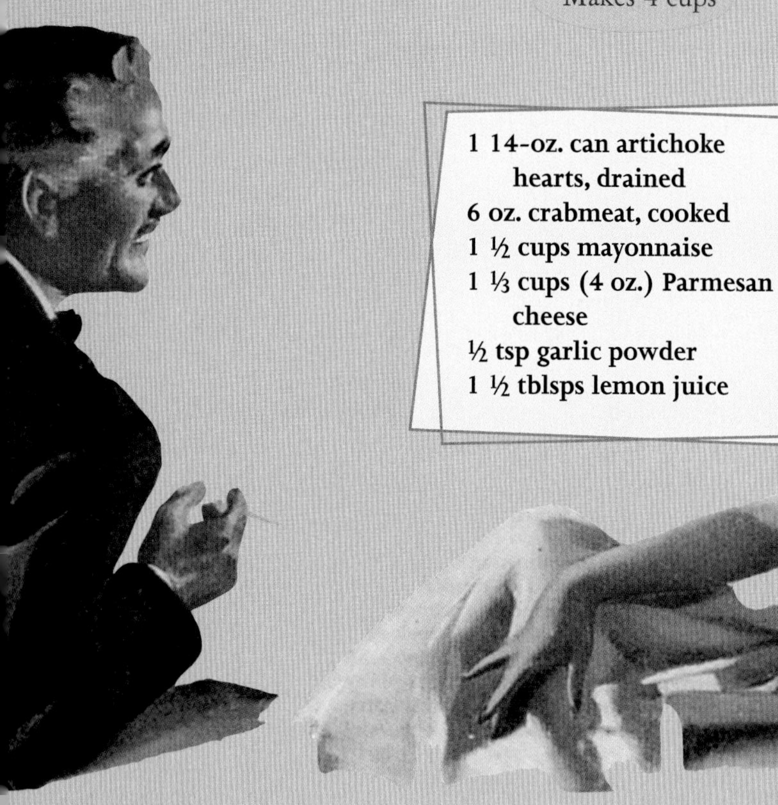

1 14-oz. can artichoke hearts, drained
6 oz. crabmeat, cooked
1 ½ cups mayonnaise
1 ⅓ cups (4 oz.) Parmesan cheese
½ tsp garlic powder
1 ½ tblsps lemon juice

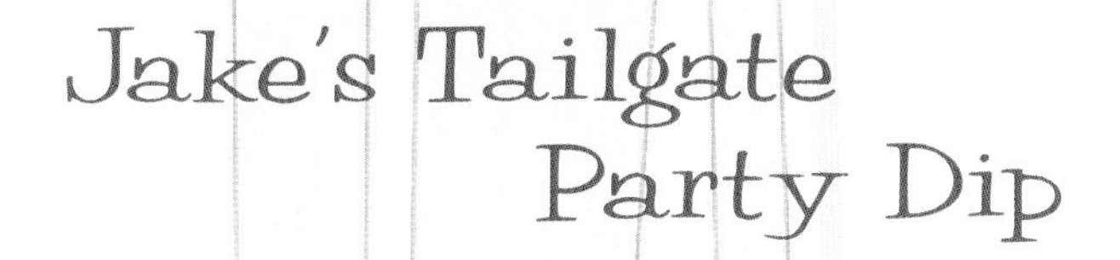

Jake's Tailgate Party Dip

2 ½ cups (10 oz.) extra-sharp cheddar cheese, shredded
½ cup beer
¼ cup mayonnaise
1 ½ tsps Worcestershire sauce
1 tsp caraway seeds
dash of salt
dash of coarsely ground black pepper

1. In a blender or food processor at medium speed blend cheese, beer, mayonnaise, Worcestershire sauce, caraway seeds, salt, and pepper. Blend until smooth.

2. Cover and refrigerate.

3. Serve with your favorite dippers, crackers, chips, or fresh veggies.

Makes 3 cups

Coronado Spread

- 1 envelope (.25-oz.) unflavored gelatin
- 1 cup cold water
- 1 cup (½ pint) sour cream
- 2 cups (8 oz.) sharp cheddar cheese, finely grated
- 1 4-oz. can diced green chilies, drained
- ¼ cup black olives, finely chopped
- 3 tblsps sweet onion, finely chopped
- 1 tsp fresh cilantro, finely chopped (or ½ tsp dried)
- dash of hot sauce (Tabasco or one of the other delightful varieties, from tastefully warm to scorching, to your taste)
- tortilla chips (offer a variety such as blue corn, white)

1. In a small saucepan sprinkle gelatin over cold water and let sit 3 or 4 minutes to soften. Over low heat stir gently until gelatin is dissolved; set aside.

2. In a medium bowl, combine sour cream and cheddar cheese. Stir in chilies, olives, onion, cilantro, and hot sauce.

3. Slowly stir in the dissolved gelatin. Refrigerate until mixture forms a mound when dropped from a spoon, about 30 to 40 minutes. Stir to evenly disperse the veggies.

4. Spoon into a 4-cup ungreased mold and refrigerate 4 to 6 hours.

5. Turn out onto serving plate and serve with a colorful medley of chips.

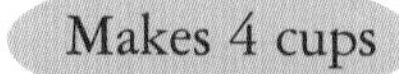

Kilauea Island Spread

1 1 ½-oz. package blue cheese, crumbled
1 8-oz. package cream cheese, softened
¼ cup macadamia nuts, finely chopped
1 tblsp crystallized ginger, finely chopped
1 8-oz. can crushed pineapple, well drained

1. In a small bowl mix blue cheese and cream cheese until smooth. Stir in nuts, ginger, and pineapple.

2. Serve with mild-flavored crackers (like water crackers), chunks of Hawaiian bread, or chunks of sweet tender rolls.

Makes 2 cups

Old Delhi Spread

1 8-oz. package cream cheese, softened
½ cup (¼ pint) sour cream
1 ½ to 2 tsps curry powder (to your taste)
dash of garlic powder
½ cup roasted peanuts, finely chopped
¼ cup raisins, finely chopped
¼ cup light raisins, finely chopped
2 slices lean bacon, cooked until crisp, drained and crumbled
2 tblsps green onions, finely chopped

1. In a medium bowl combine cream cheese, sour cream, curry powder, and garlic powder until smooth. Stir in peanuts, both raisins, and bacon until well mixed.

2. Spoon into a colorful, fun serving bowl and chill 1 hour. Garnish with green onions.

Makes 2 cups

Mukilteo ("muck-ul-tee-oh") Scoopin' Goop

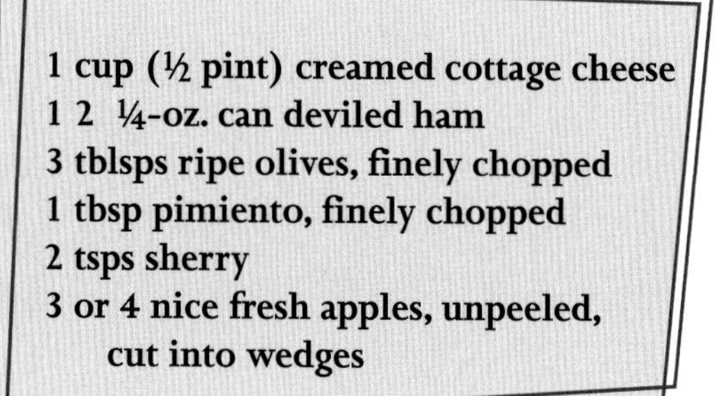

1 cup (½ pint) creamed cottage cheese
1 2 ¼-oz. can deviled ham
3 tblsps ripe olives, finely chopped
1 tbsp pimiento, finely chopped
2 tsps sherry
3 or 4 nice fresh apples, unpeeled,
cut into wedges

1. In a medium bowl combine cottage cheese, deviled ham, olives, pimiento, and sherry.

2. Mix well and heap into an attractive serving dish with apple wedges alongside as dippers. It also goes well with any crispy crackers or other dippers.

Makes 1½ cups

West Texas Caviar

3 15 ½-oz. cans black-eyed peas, rinsed and drained
½ cup bottled Italian dressing (I prefer Newman's because it's mild)
3 tsps canned jalapeno peppers, drained and finely chopped
¼ cup green pepper, finely chopped
¼ cup yellow ripe pepper, finely chopped
¼ cup red ripe pepper, finely chopped
½ cup sweet onion (Walla Walla or Vidalia), finely chopped
1 large clove garlic, finely chopped
dash of salt (or to taste)
dash of coarsely ground black pepper (or to taste)

1. In a large bowl combine black-eyed peas, dressing, all the peppers, onion, garlic, salt, and pepper.

2. Mix well and refrigerate at least 2 hours, 2 days if possible (flavors blend better).

3. Taste for salt and pepper. If mixture is a bit dry, add a little more dressing.

4. Serve in a colorful bowl with tortilla chips for dippin'.

Makes 4 cups

Poor Man's Caviar

¼ cup (½ stick) butter or margarine
1 cup (10 to 12) green onions, coarsely chopped
2 cups (about ½ pound) mushrooms, coarsely chopped
½ tsp salt
dash of coarsely ground black pepper
1 tblsp lemon juice
dash of cayenne pepper
½ cup fresh dill, chopped
½ cup sour cream

1. In a large skillet over medium heat melt butter and gently cook green onions until they become slightly transparent but not browned, about 2 minutes.

2. Add mushrooms, salt, pepper, lemon juice, and cayenne; cook 5 to 6 minutes or until mushroom juices have cooked away .

3. Cool.

4. In a small bowl combine dill and sour cream; stir in mushroom mixture. If you wish to use it as a dip, add a little more sour cream to thin the consistency.

Makes 3 cups

Dippers

If you'd like to hear "Wow! You made this yourself?" and you have the extra time and motivation, how about making your own crackers and dippers? Hey! Give it a try!

Sez-me Crackers

1 cup all-purpose flour
1 cup whole-wheat flour
¼ cup sesame seeds
½ tsp salt
¼ cup vegetable oil
½ cup water

1. Preheat oven to 350 degrees.
2. In a medium bowl combine flours with sesame seeds and salt. Make a hole in the center of the mixture and pour in oil and water. Stir until well blended.
3. Shape dough into a ball and roll out to 1/8-inch thick on a lightly floured board.
4. Cut into 2x1-inch strips and bake on ungreased cookie sheet 15 to 20 minutes or until golden brown.
5. Terrific with any dip or spread.

Makes 75 to 85 crackers

My Favorite Crunchy Nibblers

½ cup butter (yes, you can use margarine, but there is a difference in the taste)
2 cups cheddar cheese, shredded (I like sharp Tillamook)
1 package (9⁄16-oz.) dry onion soup/dip mix
1 ¼ cups all-purpose flour

Makes about 40 crackers

1. Preheat oven to 375 degrees.

2. In a large bowl, beat together butter and cheese until smooth. Stir in onion soup mix and flour. Divide in half and shape into two 5-inch rolls.

3. Wrap tightly in plastic wrap and refrigerate 3 to 4 hours. Cut rolls into 1/4-inch slices and arrange on a large greased cookie sheet.

4. Bake 10 to 12 minutes until lightly browned around the edges. Especially yummy with the Rio Grande Dip.

Thatsa Italiana! Garlic Thins

1 14- to 16-inch sourdough loaf, cocktail-style, sliced very thin (¼ inch if you can)
½ cup butter or margarine
1 clove garlic, crushed
dash of oregano
½ cup Parmesan cheese

1. Preheat oven to 300 degrees.

2. Arrange bread slices in a single layer on an ungreased cookie sheet; set aside. In a small saucepan melt butter or margarine.

3. Gradually stir in garlic and cook over medium heat until tender, about 2 minutes. Stir in oregano and cheese; remove from heat. Brush mixture over bread slices.

4. Bake about 15 minutes until crisp. Watch carefully.

Makes 60 to 65 slices

Walla Walla Cookies

3 large sweet onions (Walla Walla, Vidalia, or Maui) peeled and quartered
2 eggs
¾ cup vegetable oil
1 tblsp salt
½ cup sugar
½ cup poppy seeds
3 heaping tsps baking powder
2 ½ cups (about) all-purpose flour

1. Preheat oven to 375 degrees.

2. In your food processor or blender whirl together onions, eggs, and vegetable oil. Pour mixture into a large bowl and mix in salt, sugar, poppy seeds, and baking powder. Add enough flour so dough can be kneaded and is no longer sticky.

3. Roll out dough on a floured board and cut with a 2-inch cookie cutter. Use different shapes according to the holiday.

4. Place cookies on ungreased cookie sheets and bake until golden brown, about 10 minutes.

5. Cool on wire racks and store in an airtight container.

Makes 40 crackers

Pig Tails

¼ cup butter or margarine, softened
3 tblsps Parmesan cheese, grated
1 cup sharp Cheddar cheese, finely shredded
¼ tsp chili powder
¼ tsp celery salt
1 tsp Worcestershire sauce
dash of hot sauce (optional)
½ cup all-purpose flour

1. Preheat oven to 375 degrees.

2. In a small bowl combine butter or margarine, cheeses, chili powder, celery salt, Worcestershire sauce, and hot sauce. Beat until smooth. Stir in flour until well blended. Wrap dough in plastic wrap and refrigerate 1 hour or more.

3. Pinch off walnut-sized pieces of dough and roll between your palms to form 4-inch sticks.

4. Arrange on an ungreased cookie sheet and bake 8 to 10 minutes until golden brown. Wonderful crispy dipper with any of your favorite dips or spreads.

Makes about 30 sticks

Blue Duck Inn's French-Fried Deviled Eggs

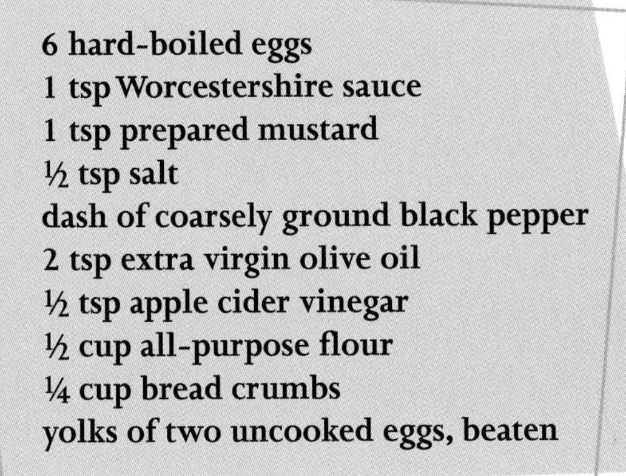

6 hard-boiled eggs
1 tsp Worcestershire sauce
1 tsp prepared mustard
½ tsp salt
dash of coarsely ground black pepper
2 tsp extra virgin olive oil
½ tsp apple cider vinegar
½ cup all-purpose flour
¼ cup bread crumbs
yolks of two uncooked eggs, beaten

1. Cut hard-boiled eggs in half and put yolks in a small bowl.

2. Mash yolks and mix well with mustard, Worcestershire sauce, salt, pepper, oil, and vinegar. Pack mixture back into the whites.

Serves 4-6

3. Put halves together and hold in place with a toothpick. Mix flour and bread crumbs in a small bowl.

4. Dip eggs in beaten egg yolks, then in flour mixture. Fry in some hot oil until golden brown.

5. Drain well on paper towels and remove toothpicks. Serve with a variety of sauces.

Creole Clementine's Ham Balls

1 pound smoked ham
1 pound lean pork (not sausage)
1/2 pound lean ground beef
2 eggs, slightly beaten
1 cup milk
1 cup soda cracker crumbs
dash of coarsely ground black pepper
1 cup brown sugar
1 tsp prepared mustard
1/2 cup water
1/2 cup apple cider vinegar (white is okay)

1. Preheat oven to 350 degrees.

2. Run ham, pork, and ground beef in your food processor until well mixed. Beat eggs with milk, just enough to blend.

3. Add egg mixture, cracker crumbs, and pepper to meat. Mix well, form into 1- to 2-inch balls, and place in a shallow baking pan.

4. In a medium saucepan heat brown sugar, mustard, water, and vinegar. Bring to a boil and pour over meat balls.

5. Bake 1 hour.

Serves 8-12

Snappy Sam's Irresistible Meatballs

2 pounds ground round
1 cup prepared cornflake crumbs
3 tblsps dried parsley flakes
2 eggs
3 tblsps soy sauce
dash of coarsely ground black pepper
½ tsp garlic powder
⅓ cup ketchup
2 tblsps dried minced onion (or 3 fresh)
1 16-oz. can jellied cranberry sauce
1 12-oz. bottle of your favorite chili sauce
3 tblsps brown sugar
2 tblsps lemon juice

1. Preheat oven to 350 degrees.

2. In a large bowl combine ground round, cornflake crumbs, parsley, eggs, soy sauce, pepper, garlic powder, ketchup, and onion. Mix well. Form into meatballs about 1 1/2-inches in diameter (the size of a walnut). Arrange meatballs in a shallow ungreased baking pan.

3. In a medium saucepan stir together cranberry sauce, chili sauce, brown sugar, and lemon juice. Cook over medium heat, stirring occasionally, until cranberry sauce is melted, about 10 minutes. Pour sauce over meatballs and bake 30 minutes.

4. Serve in a chafing dish to keep warm and provide toothpicks.

Serves 8-12

Buffalo Bart's Chicken Wings

25 chicken wings
3 to 4 cups vegetable oil
1⁄4 cup (1⁄2 stick) butter or margarine
1⁄2 to 1 2-oz. bottle Louisiana hot sauce
Blue Cheese dressing, this is traditional
(see recipe below)

Serves 6

1. Remove wing tips at "elbow" (save for chicken soup). Pour 2 1/2 to 3 inches of oil in heavy skillet and heat to 375 degrees; fry wings (nope, you do not dredge or batter first) until crisp and golden brown on all sides, 8 to 10 minutes.

2. You can also use a deep fryer. Drain well on paper towels.

3. In a small saucepan melt butter over medium-low heat and stir in hot sauce according to your taste. Remember, a full bottle is snappin' hot!

Blue Cheese Dressing

2 tblsps sweet onion, finely chopped
1 clove garlic, finely chopped
3 tblsps parsley, finely chopped
½ cup sour cream
1 cup mayonnaise
1 tblsp fresh lemon juice
1 tblsp white vinegar
⅓ cup blue cheese, crumbled
dash of salt
dash of coarsely ground black pepper
dash of cayenne (optional)

Makes 2 cups

1. In a medium bowl combine onion, garlic, parsley, sour cream, mayonnaise, lemon juice, and vinegar. Mix well.

2. Gently stir in blue cheese, salt, pepper, and cayenne, if using.

3. Serve generously with chicken wings. Garnish with celery sticks.

Rhode Island Reunion Clam Fritters

1. In a large bowl combine egg yolks, milk, and onion. Let stand 5 minutes. Stir in clams, bread crumbs, parsley, salt, pepper, and hot sauce. Fold in egg whites.

2. In a deep skillet or deep fryer heat oil to 365 degrees. Drop batter by tablespoonfuls, 4 or 5 at a time, into hot oil and fry until golden brown. Turn once.

3. Drain on paper towels. Keep hot in warm oven until ready to serve.

4. Serve with lemon wedges and tartar sauce.

2 egg yolks, well beaten
½ cup milk
1 tsp onion, finely chopped
2 6 ½-oz. cans minced clams, drained
1 cup dry bread crumbs
1 tblsp parsley, finely chopped
1 tsp salt
½ tsp coarsely ground black pepper
dash hot sauce
2 egg whites, beaten stiff
3 cups vegetable oil or shortening
lemon wedges
tartar sauce

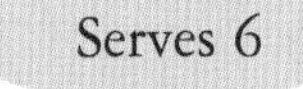
Serves 6

Baja Beach Tortilla Snacks

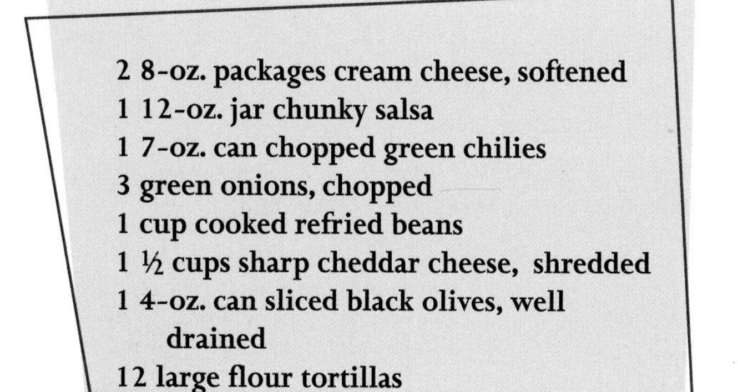

2 8-oz. packages cream cheese, softened
1 12-oz. jar chunky salsa
1 7-oz. can chopped green chilies
3 green onions, chopped
1 cup cooked refried beans
1 ½ cups sharp cheddar cheese, shredded
1 4-oz. can sliced black olives, well drained
12 large flour tortillas

1. In your food processor or mixer bowl combine cream cheese, salsa, green chilies, onions, and refried beans. Mix until smooth. Stir in cheese and olives.

2. Spread on tortillas and roll to enclose filling. Wrap in plastic wrap and chill. One hour before serving cut tortillas into 1 1/2-inch sections.

3. Warm before serving and add toothpicks.

Serves 12-15

Boise Babe's Tater Skins

Variations:

- Monterey Jack cheese with jalapeno peppers
- Sharp Cheddar with a little Walla Walla sweet onion

4 large Idaho baking potatoes
2 tblsps butter, softened
1⁄2 tsp salt
1⁄2 tsp coarsely ground black pepper
1 cup (about 1⁄4 pound) Monterey Jack cheese, finely shredded
4 slices lean pepper bacon, cooked crisp and crumbled

Serves 4

1. Preheat oven to 375 degrees.

2. Stick potatoes several times with a fork and bake until tender, about 1 hour. Halve lengthwise and scoop out flesh, leaving shell with a 3/8-inch-thick layer. (Save scooped-out innards for soup or mashed potatoes.) Butter insides of shells, sprinkle with salt and pepper, then slice each half into thirds.

3. Arrange potato skins butter side up and sprinkle with cheese and bacon. Broil 5 inches below heat just until cheese melts, about 2 minutes.

Baked Tater Party

1 large Idaho baker per guest. Scrub gently but thoroughly. Dry. Pierce potato with a fork in several places. Bake in 425-degree oven about 55 to 60 minutes or until soft or, cook in a microwave 4 to 5 minutes per potato.

For a different taste try rubbing potato with a flavored butter or oil. You can also add one or more of the following spices or herbs to vegetable oil or butter: garlic powder, onion powder, celery salt, cayenne, paprika, freshly ground black pepper, basil, thyme, marjoram, dry mustard, or prepared flavored mustard (try honey or hot).

Use some of the following toppings:

- Sour cream
- Salsa (mild and hot)
- Real butter, margarine, or yogurt spread
- Chives, green onions, sweet Walla Walla onions; finely chopped or thinly sliced red onions
- Melted cheese (microwave American processed cheese); cheese with jalapenos
- Bacon, cooked crisp and crumbled
- Cooked ham cut in bite-sized pieces; offer with cheese or mix with melted cheese
- Canned corned beef hash, cooked and offered with poached eggs
- Potato Benedict: Canadian bacon, poached egg, and Hollandaise sauce
- Chopped olives: ripe, Italian, Greek, stuffed green
- Broccoli flowerets, sliced zucchini, snow peas, mushrooms; all cooked crisp-tender
- Frozen chopped spinach, cooked, drained well, and mixed with sour cream and bacon bits

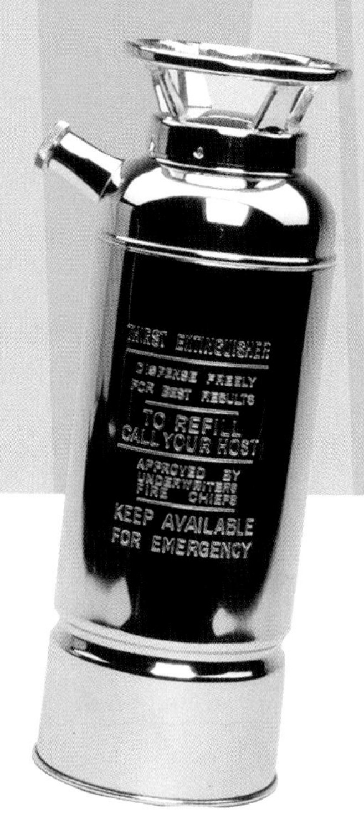

- Sausage, mild or hot, cooked, drained on paper towels, and crumbled
- Leftover steak cut into 1/4-inch-thick strips
- Leftover or canned chili con carne, with or without beans
- Hot crab or shrimp filling
- Country gravy, with or without sausage
- A selection of chopped chilies, from mild to hot
- Pizza sauce; offer with shredded mozzarella or Parmesan
  or canned beef stew
- Crumbled blue cheese, shredded sharp Cheddar,
  crumbled Feta
- Frozen veggies in butter or cream sauce, cooked per
  package directions
- Canned French-fried onions
- Flavored cream cheeses
- Marinated vegetable salad from your deli
- Hot sauerkraut and pastrami for a Reuben potato
- Leftover pot roast and gravy; stir in sour cream
  before serving
- Leftover cooked chicken or turkey with its own gravy
  or in a cream sauce
- Hard-cooked eggs chopped; offer as a sprinkle-on
  topping or in a white sauce or mild cheese sauce
- Stir-fried veggie combinations, with or without meat.
- Scrambled eggs: toss with leftover crumbled bacon,
  bits of cooked or smoked salmon, ham, or chives
- Chopped avocado
- Canned tuna, salmon, shrimp, or crabmeat in a
  cream or light cheese sauce

Mona Lisa's Hometown Olives

½ pound green olives, the pitted variety
½ pound black olives, ditto
¼ cup extra virgin olive oil (unless you prefer one stronger in flavor)
¼ cup white vinegar
3 celery stalks, chopped
1 green pepper, chopped
1 red pepper, chopped (or for more color use ½ each red and yellow)
2 garlic cloves, crushed
dash or two of freshly ground black pepper
dash of oregano

1. In a large glass jar or bowl combine olives, olive oil, vinegar, celery, peppers, garlic, black pepper, and oregano. Mix well, cover, and let sit on your counter at room temperature 2 days.

2. Store in refrigerator.

Serves 8-10

Aristocratic Artichokes

12 oz. package frozen artichoke hearts
2 pounds small mushrooms
1 tsp salt
¼ tsp dry mustard
½ tsp cayenne pepper
¼ cup apple cider vinegar
1 tblsp lemon juice
1 cup salad oil or olive oil
3 cloves of garlic, finely chopped
(or 3 tsps minced garlic from a jar)
dash of hot sauce

1. In a medium saucepan or steamer cook artichokes until tender, about 12 minutes.

2. Drain and chill. Slice mushrooms in half through stems.

3. In a quart glass jar with a lid (like a canning jar) shake together salt, mustard, cayenne pepper, vinegar, lemon juice, oil, garlic, and hot sauce. Toss together 'chokes and 'shrooms and pour dressing over them.

4. Cover and refrigerate 4 to 8 hours. Stir a few times. Drain before serving.

Serves 8-10

Blue Velvet

1 8-oz. package cream cheese, softened
1 4-oz. package blue cheese, crumbled
¾ tsp dry mustard
2 ½ tsps bourbon
3 tblsps toasted sesame seeds

1. In the small bowl of your mixer beat cream cheese and blue cheese until well blended. Beat in mustard and bourbon.

2. Shape cheese mixture into a ball, wrap with plastic wrap, and refrigerate overnight. Before serving, unwrap ball and roll in sesame seeds.

3. Serve with an assortment of crackers.

Mad Russian Rick's Appeteasers

1 8-oz. package cream cheese, softened
1 ½ cups all-purpose flour
½ cup butter or margarine (butter's better)
½ pound ground beef
1 medium onion, finely chopped
¼ cup water
¼ cup sour cream
½ tsp dill weed
1 egg, hard-boiled and chopped
½ tsp salt
dash or two of coarsely ground black pepper
1 egg, well-beaten

1. In a medium bowl knead together cream cheese, flour, and butter or margarine until mixture is smooth. Shape dough into a ball, wrap in plastic wrap, and refrigerate at least 1 hour.

2. In a medium skillet cook ground beef and onion together until meat is browned and onion is transparent. Remove from heat. Stir in water, sour cream, dill, chopped egg, salt, and pepper.

3. On a lightly floured surface use a floured rolling pin and roll out unwrapped dough to about 1/8-inch thick. With a 2 3/4-inch round cookie cutter (or a small juice glass or anything similar), cut out rounds.

4. Place 1 tsp of the meat mixture on one-half of each round. Brush edge of round with beaten egg, fold dough over the meat mixture, and press edges together with a fork. Place on ungreased cookie sheet. If you aren't serving these immediately cover and refrigerate.

5. About 25 minutes before serving, heat oven to 425 degrees and bake pastries until golden brown, about 10 minutes.

6. Serve hot.

Serves 15-20

Taj Mahal Chicken Pockets

2 tblsps butter or margarine
2 tblsps onion, finely chopped
2 tsps curry powder
2 tblsps all-purpose flour
½ tsp salt
¾ cup milk
1 6 ¾- oz. can chunk chicken, drained
1 10- to 11-oz. package piecrust mix
1 egg, slightly beaten

Serves 6-8

1. In a medium saucepan melt butter or margarine over medium heat. Add onion and curry and cook until onion is transparent, about 5 minutes. Stir in flour and salt until well blended, about 1 minute. Gradually stir in milk and continue stirring until mixture is thick and smooth, about 5 minutes. Remove from heat and stir in chicken.

2. Prepare piecrust as directed on label. Follow directions for rolling out, cutting, and forming into pockets as described in Mad Russian Rick's Appeteasers, p. 63.

3. About 35 minutes before serving, preheat oven to 400 degrees and bake 25 minutes or until golden brown. Serve hot.

Wisconsonite Party Bake

4 cups cracker crumbs
1 cup butter or margarine, melted
½ tsp curry powder
2 cups sweet Walla Walla or Vidalia onions, finely chopped
½ tsp salt (or to taste)
1 ½ cups cheddar cheese, shredded (I prefer sharp Tillamook)
3 cups milk, scalded
3 eggs, lightly beaten
1 tsp salt
dash of cayenne pepper
¾ cup Parmesan cheese, grated
1 tsp paprika

1. Preheat oven to 375 degrees.

2. In a medium bowl combine cracker crumbs, melted butter, and curry powder. Press 3/4 of the mixture into an 11x16-inch baking dish. Spread onions over crumb mixture; sprinkle with salt (or to taste) and cheddar cheese.

3. In a medium bowl combine milk, eggs, 1 tsp salt, and cayenne; mix well. Spoon over cheddar cheese. Top with reserved crumb mixture, Parmesan cheese, and paprika. Bake 25 minutes. Cut into 2-inch squares.

Serves 15-20

La-Dee-Dah Crepes

Filling

Serves 6-8

- 1 pound lean bacon
- 1 cup cheddar cheese, grated (I prefer sharp Tillamook)
- ½ cup sour cream
- 1 3-oz. package cream cheese, softened
- ½ pound pastrami, thinly sliced
- 3 tblsps mayonnaise
- ¼ cup celery, finely chopped
- 2 tblsps fresh parsley, finely chopped (or 3 tblsps dried), divided
- 8 drops hot sauce
- dash of Worcestershire sauce
- ½ tsp dry mustard
- 3 fresh green onions, finely chopped

1. In a medium skillet cook bacon until crisp; drain on paper towels and crumble.

2. In a large mixing bowl combine cheddar cheese, sour cream, cream cheese, pastrami, mayonnaise, celery, 1 tblsp parsley, hot sauce, Worcestershire sauce, mustard, and onions.

3. Mix well.

Crepes

2 eggs
1 tsp salt
1 cup flour
1 cup beer
1 tblsp sour cream
1 tblsp butter

1. In a medium bowl use your mixer to beat together eggs and salt. Gradually mix in flour, alternating with beer. Beat until smooth.

2. Stir in sour cream and butter. Refrigerate batter 1 hour. Cook on crepe pan, griddle, or skillet until crepe shows bubbles, then turn and cook until light brown. Crepe should be about 6 inches in diameter.

3. Place each crepe on a plate, spoon on 1 tablespoon filling, roll. Garnish with remaining parsley.

Hoowee Loowee's Crepes Supreme

Crepes

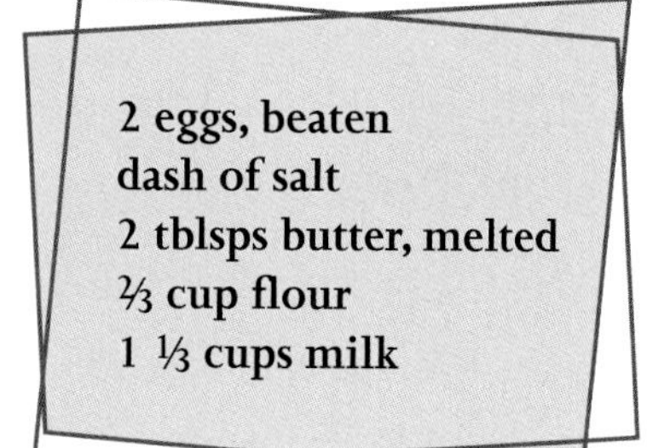

2 eggs, beaten
dash of salt
2 tblsps butter, melted
⅔ cup flour
1 ⅓ cups milk

1. In a medium bowl beat eggs until foamy; add salt and butter. Mix in flour and milk, beat.

2. Cook as described in La-Dee-Dah Crepes, p. 67.

- 5 ounces Italian sausage
- 1 clove garlic, crushed
- 1 ½ packages frozen spinach
- 1 cup cooked chicken, chopped
- ¾ cup Parmesan cheese, grated
- 1 tsp onion salt

1. In a medium skillet cook sausage with garlic. Break up sausage with a fork and drain off fat. In a saucepan cook spinach according to package directions; drain well and add to sausage. Add chicken, Parmesan cheese, and onion salt.

2. Place a tablespoon or so of filling in each crepe, roll up, and secure with a toothpick. Place in a baking dish.

Sauce

6 tblsps butter
6 tblsps flour
3 cups heavy cream
2 cups Parmesan cheese, grated
1 tsp onion, grated
dash of curry powder

1. Preheat oven to 350 degrees.
2. In a saucepan melt butter over medium low heat. Stir in flour. Gradually whisk in cream; stir until mixture thickens and is smooth. Add Parmesan cheese, onion, and curry.
3. Pour over crepes and bake 20 minutes.

Serves 6-8

It's Greek to Me!

1 pound feta cheese
1 8-oz. package cream cheese, softened
1 pint large curd cottage cheese
3 eggs
2 tblsps fresh parsley, finely chopped
dash of cayenne pepper
¾ pound filo dough
1 cup butter, melted

1. Preheat oven to 350 degrees.

2. In your food processor or blender mix feta cheese, cream cheese, cottage cheese, eggs, parsley, and pepper. Whirl together until smooth. Lay out filo, one sheet at a time, and brush with melted butter. Cut each sheet into 2-inch-wide strips.

3. Place a heaping teaspoon of filling on one end of the strip and fold over one corner to make a triangle. Cut pastry.

4. Continue this process until all strips are used. Place on a buttered baking sheet and bake 15 minutes, or until golden brown. These freeze well.

Makes about 72

Bolinhas de Bacalhau

(Portuguese Codfish Balls)

⅓ cup sweet onion, finely chopped
2 tblsps virgin olive oil
10 oz. dried salt cod
1 quart boiling water
1 large baking potato (about ½ pound), unpeeled
1 cup milk
2 tblsps parsley, finely chopped
dash of coarsely ground black pepper
2 eggs
5 cups vegetable oil

1. In a small bowl mix onion and olive oil. Set aside.

2. Rinse cod several times under cold running water. Cut into 2-inch chunks and place in a heat-proof bowl. Pour boiling water over fish and let stand 30 minutes.

3. In a small saucepan boil unpeeled potato until tender, drain, and cool until you can handle it. Peel and break potato into small chunks. Blot dry on paper towels and mash.

4. Drain cod, rinse well in cool water, and return to bowl. Pour in hot milk and and let stand another 30 minutes. Drain and discard milk. Crumble cod until fine and fluffy.

5. Return cod to bowl, add onion mixture, mashed potatoes, parsley, and pepper. Beat together until well blended. Add eggs and continue beating until mixture is smooth and light.

6. In a heavy skillet heat oil on high to 375 degrees. Use two teaspoons to scoop a heaping teaspoon of cod mixture and form into a ball. Drop into hot oil and fry until browned, about 2 to 3 minutes. Don't overcrowd in skillet.

7. Drain on paper towels and serve hot.

Makes about 25

Stormwatcher's Clam Crisps

Throwing a party to watch a spectacular Pacific storm is popular here on the peninsula. Clam digging is also a favorite pastime. Combine the two and it's a great party!

4 tblsps sweet onion, finely chopped
1 tblsp butter
5 tsps all-purpose flour
1 cup clams, minced
½ cup clam liquid
¼ tsp Worcestershire sauce
¼ tsp garlic powder
12 slices white bread, crusts removed
3 tblsps butter, softened
1 tblsp butter, melted

1. Preheat oven to 425 degrees.

2. In a medium skillet gently cook the onion in 1 tblsp butter until tender. Stir in flour. Add clams, clam liquid, Worcestershire sauce, and garlic powder. Cook 2 minutes or until thickened, stirring constantly. Cool.

3. Flatten bread with a rolling pin. Cover each slice with a light spread of softened butter, then a layer of clam filling.

4. Roll up bread to enclose filling and secure with toothpicks. Place on baking sheet and brush lightly with melted butter.

5. Bake 8 to 10 minutes or until golden brown. Serve hot.

Serves 12

Bayou Biloxi Shrimp

1 pound medium size shrimp, shelled and deveined
¼ cup butter or margarine
2 tblsps lemon juice
dash of salt
dash of coarsely ground black pepper
3 tblsps barbecue sauce
1 garlic clove, smashed
1 bay leaf, crumbled
½ tsp crushed dried red peppers
½ tsp dried basil leaves
½tsp dried rosemary leaves
½ tsp paprika

1. Butterfly shrimp by cutting lengthwise down back but not cutting all the way through.

2. In a large skillet melt butter or margarine, add shrimp, and cook 3 to 4 minutes or until shrimp starts to turn pink.

3. Add lemon juice, salt, pepper, barbecue sauce, garlic, bay leaf, red peppers, basil, rosemary, and paprika. Simmer over low heat another 5 minutes, stirring occasionally.

4. Cover and let stand about 5 minutes. Serve with toothpicks to spear these luscious treats.

Serves 8-10

The Grand Finale

Perhaps a sweet treat will fit your party plans rather than appetizers, dips, or such. Or, you might like to finish off a fun evening with dessert. Here are a few delights proven to gather in the ooohs, aaahs, and Gee!-you-shouldn't-haves.

Jamaican Banana Cake

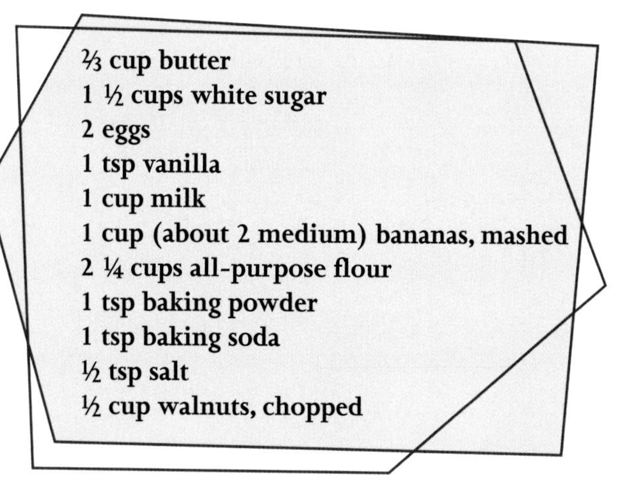

⅔ cup butter
1 ½ cups white sugar
2 eggs
1 tsp vanilla
1 cup milk
1 cup (about 2 medium) bananas, mashed
2 ¼ cups all-purpose flour
1 tsp baking powder
1 tsp baking soda
½ tsp salt
½ cup walnuts, chopped

1. Preheat oven to 350 degrees. Grease and lightly flour a 13x9x2-inch baking pan or nonstick pan.

2. In a large bowl cream together butter, sugar, eggs, and vanilla. Beat at medium speed until light and fluffy. Add milk, mashed bananas, flour, baking powder, baking soda, and salt. Beat on low until well blended. Beat at medium speed 3 minutes more.

3. Stir in nuts and pour into pan.

4. Bake 40 to 45 minutes until golden brown. Poke center with a toothpick and it should come out clean. Cool 5 minutes.

Serves 6-8

Jamaican Banana Cake Topping

⅓ cup butter
¼ cup brown sugar, firmly packed
2 tblsps milk
1 cup flaked coconut
½ cup pecans, chopped
(walnuts are okay)

1. Preheat broiler.

2. In a small saucepan combine butter, brown sugar, and milk and cook over medium heat, stirring often, until mixture boils. Stir in coconut and nuts.

3. Spread over the warm cake. Broil 4 inches from the heat 2 to 3 minutes or until golden brown. Watch closely so it doesn't scorch! Cool.

Traditional Pound Cake

3 cups all-purpose flour
¼ tsp salt
1 tsp baking powder
1 tsp ground mace
2 cups (4 sticks) real butter
2 cups white sugar
9 eggs, separated
2 tblsps cognac
fresh or frozen fruit such as
strawberries, blueberries, peaches
or canned fruit topping
whipped cream or vanilla ice cream

1. Preheat oven to 350 degrees for 30 minutes.

2. Grease and lightly flour a 10-inch tube pan or use a nonstick pan.

3. Sift together flour, salt, baking powder, and mace. Set aside.

4. In a medium bowl use your mixer and cream butter, then add sugar a little at a time until mixture is smooth.

5. Beat egg yolks and stir into creamed mixture. Add flour mixture a little at a time, stirring until smooth. Whip egg whites into stiff peaks and fold into batter with cognac.

6. Pour into pan and bake 35 minutes at 350 degrees, then reduce heat to 325 degrees and continue baking another 25 minutes or until toothpick poked in center comes out clean. Let stand 10 minutes before turning out of pan.

7. To serve, offer your guests a variety of toppings and a bowl of whipped cream to garnish the top.

Serves 6-8

Boracho (Drunken) Bananas

2 cups water
½ cup brown sugar
½ cup white sugar
2 slices lemon with rind
4 slices orange with rind
1 tsp rum extract
6 large ripe bananas
¼ cup butter (no margarine!)
3 oz. (6 tblsps) Jamaican rum

1. In a medium saucepan boil water, brown sugar, white sugar, and lemon and orange slices until mixture comes to light candy stage (245 degrees or forms a sheet if you dribble a little off a spoon). Add rum extract. Split bananas lengthwise.

2. In a medium skillet melt butter, add bananas, and sauté' until lightly browned.

3. Serve with sauce spooned over bananas, then sprinkle a teaspoon of rum over each half.

Serves 6-8

Crispy Critter

Here's a quick dessert you can toss together and bake while visiting with unexpected guests. Keep a few cans of fruit pie filling on hand.

1. Preheat oven to 375 degrees.

2. Pour pie filling into greased or nonstick 8-inch-square baking pan. In a medium bowl combine rolled oats, brown sugar, flour, cinnamon, and nutmeg. Cut in butter with a fork. Sprinkle mixture over filling.

3. Bake about 30 minutes or until golden brown.

4. Serve warm with whipped cream or a dollop of vanilla ice cream.

Serves 6-8

1 21-oz.. can cherry, apple, peach, or other filling
¾ cup quick-cooking rolled oats
⅔ cup brown sugar, firmly packed
½ cup all-purpose flour
¾ tsp ground cinnamon
dash of nutmeg
½ cup butter or margarine
whipped cream or vanilla ice cream

Lemon Kiss Party Cake

This is a great party cake because you can make it a day, or even two, ahead, except for the frosting.

1 envelope (.25-oz.) unflavored gelatin
¼ cup cold water
6 eggs, separated
1 ½ cups white sugar, divided
2 tsp grated lemon peel
¾ cup lemon juice
1 10-inch angel food cake, either bought or baked yourself
1 cup heavy cream
1 tblsp confectioner's sugar

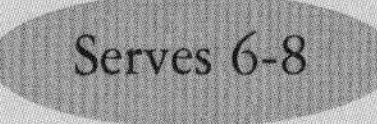
Serves 6-8

1. Soften gelatin in cold water.
2. In a medium saucepan beat egg yolks. Add 3/4 cup sugar, lemon peel, and lemon juice. Cook over low heat, stirring constantly until mixture thickens. Remove from heat, add gelatin, and stir until dissolved. Cool.
3. Brush any brown crumbs off cake surface. Crumble cake into bite-size pieces. Beat egg whites until soft peaks form.
4. Gradually add 3/4 cup sugar, beating until stiff peaks form. Fold cooled custard mixture into egg whites.
5. Pour a layer of custard in bottom of a buttered 10-inch tube pan, then continue alternating with cake ending with custard. Refrigerate at least 6 hours, or preferably overnight, until firm. Unmold on platter.
6. In a small bowl whip cream with confectioner's sugar and spread over cake.

Quenchers

Chapter 3

WHETHER IT'S A summertime blast on the beach or a sundown bash on your deck - cool, frosty, and fun are the words for satisfying everyone's thirst.

Cool Man Cool!

Julius Caesar

⅔ cup (6 oz.) frozen orange juice concentrate
1 cup whole milk
1 cup water
½ cup white sugar
1 tsp vanilla
10 - 12 ice cubes

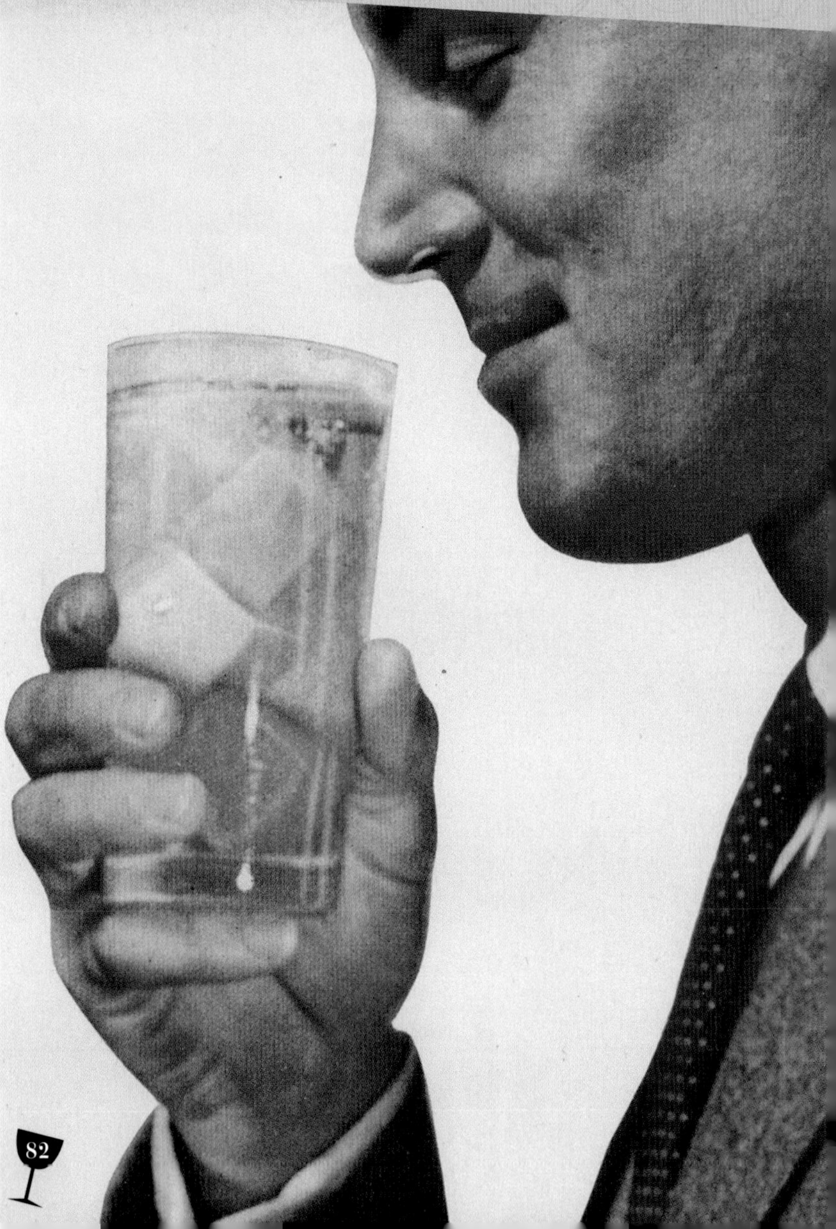

1. Combine orange juice, milk, water, sugar, vanilla, and ice cubes in blender (if you don't have a large blender you may have to do this by halves).

2. Cover and blend on medium speed until smooth, about 30 seconds. Serve immediately.

Makes 4 servings

Chilled Out Syllabub

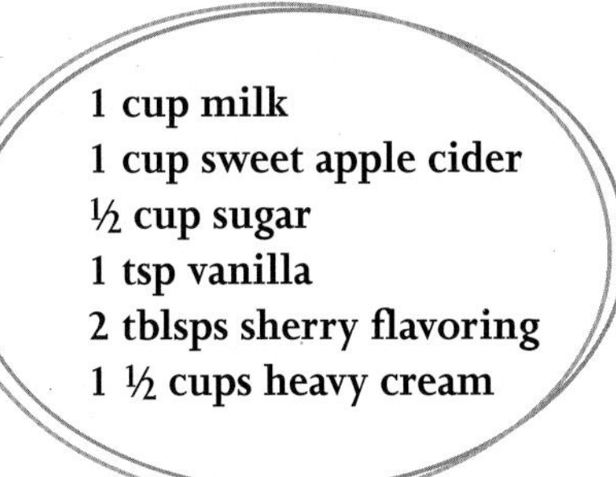
1 cup milk
1 cup sweet apple cider
½ cup sugar
1 tsp vanilla
2 tblsps sherry flavoring
1 ½ cups heavy cream

1. In your blender combine milk, cider, sugar, vanilla, and sherry flavoring. In a deep chilled bowl whip cream until slightly thickened.

2. Add to milk mixture. Put in freezer until ice crystals form.

3. Serve in tall, frosted, elegant glasses.

Makes 6 servings

Waimea Grass Skirt Cooler

(All juices should be chilled to almost freezing.)
1 cup pineapple juice
1 cup orange juice
½ cup lime juice
¼ cup lemon juice
½ cup sugar (or to taste)
1 pint (2 cups) vanilla ice cream

1. Blend juices with sugar in a blender or mix well with a whip.

2. Add ice cream and beat until smooth. Garnish each glass with a thin slice of lemon, lime, or orange.

Makes 4 servings

Dixieland Jazzle

Makes 6 servings

5 cups white sugar
7 cups water
5 bananas, well mashed
1⅔ cups orange juice
1 cup lemon juice
lemon/lime carbonated beverage

1. In a large saucepan combine sugar and water and bring to a boil over medium high heat. Stir constantly until sugar is dissolved. Cook 5 minutes.

2. In a separate bowl combine sugar syrup, bananas, and orange and lemon juices. Mix well and pour into a freezer container.

3. Freeze until mixture becomes slushy.

4. Spoon mixture into 6 tall frosted glasses and finish filling with lemon/lime beverage.

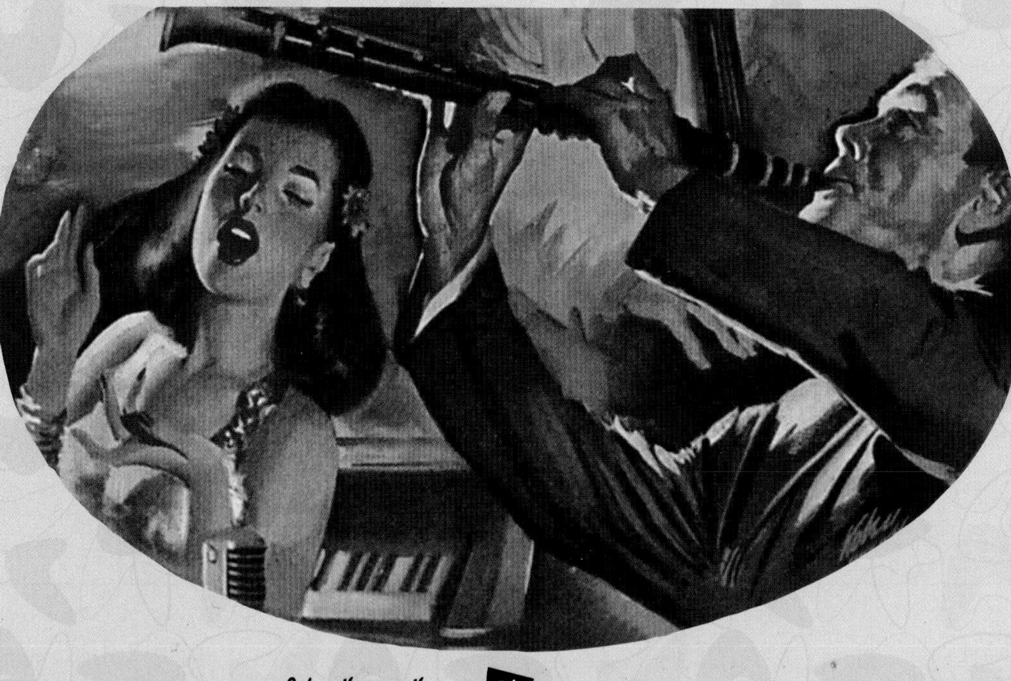

Drum Point Inn's Rassleberry Shrub

(Southerners call any slushy frozen drink a "shrub")

1 10-oz. package frozen raspberries in syrup
¼ cup red wine vinegar
water or club soda
fresh mint leaves (optional)

1. Run raspberries for 30 seconds in your blender or food processor. Bring vinegar to a boil and pour over raspberries.

2. Whir until smooth. Run through a strainer. Place in freezer until mixture becomes thick and slushy.

3. To serve, dilute to taste with about 1 part water or club soda to 2 parts shrub.

4. Garnish each glass with a mint leaf, if desired.

Makes 6 to 8 servings

Rock-Around-the-Clock Party Slush

¾ cup white sugar
1 cup hot strong Orange Pekoe tea
1 6-oz. can frozen lemonade con centrate, thawed
1 6-oz. can frozen orange juice concentrate, thawed
8 cups cold water
1 2-liter bottle lemon/lime carbonated beverage

1. In a gallon container dissolve sugar in hot tea. Mix tea with thawed lemonade and orange juice. Add water and mix until well blended.

2. Place in freezer until mixture is slushy.

3. Fill each glass half full with slush, then fill with carbonated beverage.

Makes 6 to 8 servings

Lahaina Luau

1 pint (2 cups) vanilla ice cream, slightly softened
1 pint (2 cups) lemon sherbert, slightly softened
2 cups canned pineapple juice
2 tblsps lemon juice
2 tblsps grated lemon rind, divided
2 cups ginger ale
4 to 6 pineapple chunks

1. In a large bowl combine ice cream, sherbert, pineapple juice, lemon juice, and 1 tblsp lemon rind..
2. With your hand mixer beat at low speed until foamy.
3. Add ginger ale. Beat again until foamy. Serve in chilled glasses.
4. Garnish with pineapple chunks and remaining lemon rind.

Makes approximately 1/2 gallon

Cranana Chiller

4 ripe bananas, peeled and sliced
4 cups chilled cranberry juice cocktail
1 pint (2 cups) vanilla ice cream

1. Whirl sliced bananas in blender until smooth.

2. Beat in cranberry juice and vanilla ice cream.

3. Serve in tall chilled glass.

Makes 4 servings

Gold Coast Cooler

- 1 cup chilled orange juice
- ½ cup chilled lime juice
- ¼ cup chilled lemon juice
- 1 cup chilled pineapple juice
- ½ cup sugar syrup
- 1 pint (2 cups) vanilla ice cream
- thin slices of orange, lemon, and lime

1. In your blender whirl together orange, lime, lemon, and pineapple juices with sugar syrup.
2. Add ice cream and beat just until well blended.
3. Pour into tall glasses and garnish with citrus slices.

Makes 4 servings

Sugar Syrup

1. Heat equal parts of sugar and water until sugar dissolves.

Ambrosia

- 4 ripe bananas, sliced
- ⅓ cup orange juice
- 6 tblsps honey
- dash of salt
- ½ tsp almond extract
- 1 quart cold milk

1. In your blender whirl bananas until smooth. Add orange juice, honey, salt, and almond extract; blend well.
2. Add milk and continue blending until smooth and creamy.

Makes 6 servings

Flip-Flop Fizzee

1 12-oz. can (1 ½ cups)
apricot nectar
¼ cup lemon juice
1 tblsp sugar
1 cup ginger ale
1 cup crushed ice

1. In your blender whirl together apricot nectar, lemon juice, sugar, ginger ale, and ice.
2. Blend until frothy.
3. Pour immediately into chilled glasses.

Makes 4 to 6 serving

Boca-Roca Floridian Cooler

1 6-oz. can frozen lemonade concentrate, slightly thawed
1 6-oz. can frozen orange juice concentrate, slightly thawed
2 ½ cups crushed ice
1 tsp sugar
2 cups club soda
1 fresh orange, sliced thin
1 fresh lemon, sliced thin

1. In your blender whirl together lemonade and orange juice.
2. Add ice and blend until mixture is slushy. Add sugar and continue to blend until mixture is foamy.
3. Pour into large chilled glass pitcher and stir in club soda.
4. Serve in frosty wine glasses. Garnish with an orange and lemon slice.

Makes 4 servings

Captain Cook's Kealakekua Chiller

¼ cup sugar syrup (see recipe on page 88)
1 12-oz. can mango nectar
1 6-oz. can frozen tropical punch, slightly thawed
6 cups fresh pineapple chunks, divided
¼ cup lemon juice
tropical drink umbrellas

1. In your blender whirl sugar syrup, mango nectar, punch, 5 cups pineapple chunks, and lemon juice. Blend until smooth.
2. Place in large bowl and freeze until slushy; whisk about every 30 minutes.
3. Remove and fill glasses; garnish each with a pineapple chunk and one of those little umbrellas.

Variation: Instead of using tropical punch and lemon juice, try 1 banana, 3 tblsps cream of coconut, and 2 cups crushed ice.

Makes approximately 1 gallon

Rosy Princess

2 cups fresh strawberries, plus more for garnish
2 cups watermelon, seeded and cut in chunks
¼ cup sugar syrup (see recipe on page 88)
3 tblsps lemon juice
1-2 cups crushed ice

1. In your blender combine strawberries, watermelon, sugar syrup, lemon juice, and crushed ice. Whirl until smooth.

2. Pour into glasses and garnish each with a fresh strawberry.

Makes 4 to 6 servings

Gramma's Real Summertime Lemonade

2 cups fresh-squeezed lemon juice
4 tsps grated lemon rind
1 ½ cups granulated sugar
ice cubes
cold water
thin lemon slices or fresh mint sprigs

1. In a glass canning jar (or a similar covered pitcher) combine lemon juice, lemon rind, and sugar.

2. Stir until sugar is dissolved.

3. Refrigerate.

To serve: Fill tall glass with ice cubes, pour 1/4 cup lemonade mixture over ice, fill glass with cold water. Stir. Garnish with lemon slice or mint sprig.

Makes 8-10 servings

Red Dawn

2 ½ cups tomato juice
2 tblsps lemon juice
2 tsps Worcestershire sauce
3 tsps sweet onion, grated
½ cup cucumber, grated
½ tsp celery salt
dash of cayenne pepper
ice

1. Combine tomato juice, lemon juice, Worcestershire sauce, onion, cucumber, celery salt, and cayenne in your blender and whirl 30 seconds.

2. Place in a glass pitcher or jar and refrigerate at least 2 hours.

3. Just before serving add 6 ice cubes and shake well.

Makes 4-6 servings

Wake-up Call

5 cups tomato juice
½ tsp horseradish (1 tsp if you like it a bit hotter)
2 tsps Worcestershire sauce
2 tsps lemon juice
1 tsp salt
½ tsp celery salt
3 tsps sweet onion, grated

1. In a glass pitcher combine tomato juice, horseradish, Worcestershire sauce, lemon juice, salt, celery salt, and onion.

2. Refrigerate overnight (if possible). Strain before serving.

Variation: Combine equal parts tomato juice with clam juice.

Makes about 8 servings

Ya Coulda Fooled Me Champagne Punch

8 cups pineapple juice (chilled almost to freezing)
2 32-oz. bottles nonalcoholic white wine
1 32-oz. bottle nonalcoholic champagne
1 6-oz. can frozen lemonade concentrate, thawed
maraschino cherries
crushed ice

1. In your punch bowl mix well pineapple juice, white wine, champagne, and lemonade.
2. Add crushed ice and garnish with maraschino cherries.

Makes about 36 servings

Buckin' Bronc Punch

4 quarts (1 gallon) strong, flavorful coffee
1 quart heavy cream
5 tblsps white sugar
4 tsps vanilla
2 quarts (1 half-gallon) vanilla ice cream, slightly softened
¼ oz. baker's milk or semi-sweet chocolate

1. Refrigerate coffee. In a medium bowl whip cream until stiff, gradually adding sugar and vanilla.
2. Spoon ice cream into your punch bowl; add whipped cream, then pour cooled coffee over all.
3. Mix well, but gently. Grate a little chocolate over the top.

Makes about 36 servings

Pink Peach Plantation Punch

1 20-oz. can peach halves
crushed ice
1 46-oz. can peach nectar
2 quarts ginger ale, well chilled
¼ cup lime juice
fresh mint leaves

1. Run peach halves in your blender on high speed 30 seconds.
2. Place enough crushed ice in your punch bowl to fill it 1/4 full.
3. Pour in nectar, blended peaches, ginger ale, and lime juice; mix well.
4. Garnish with a few mint leaves.

Makes 1 gallon

Scarlett O'Hara's Plantation Tea

Per serving:

1 ½ tsps fine Orange Pekoe tea per cup
ice cubes or crushed ice
½ cup fresh mint leaves (sorry, dried won't do)
2 medium lemons, sliced very thin
fresh mint sprigs
sugar (optional)

1. For each cup you want to brew use 1 ½ tsps tea. Steep 10 minutes.
2. Cool slightly.
3. Fill a large glass pitcher with ice and mint leaves. Pour tea over ice and mint.
4. Serve each glass with a garnish of lemon slice and sprig of mint. Offer sugar to sweeten if desired.

Rio De Café

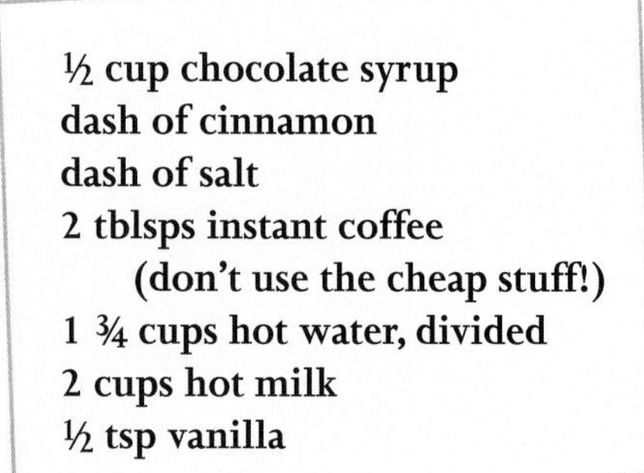

½ cup chocolate syrup
dash of cinnamon
dash of salt
2 tblsps instant coffee
(don't use the cheap stuff!)
1 ¾ cups hot water, divided
2 cups hot milk
½ tsp vanilla

1. In a medium saucepan combine chocolate syrup, cinnamon, salt, coffee, vanilla, and 1/4 cup hot water.

2. Warm over medium heat until heated through; stir often.

3. Add milk and 1 1/2 cups hot water, stirring often until heated through.

4. Beat with a hand mixer until foamy. Serve immediately.

Makes 4-6 servings

Northern Lights Coffee

1 cup rich milk
1 cup whipping cream
1 tsp white sugar
dash of vanilla
2 cups freshly brewed strong coffee
French vanilla ice cream

1. Combine milk, cream, sugar, and vanilla in a medium glass bowl or microwave-safe pitcher.
2. Heat in microwave 1 minute.
3. Stir. Return to microwave 1 minute longer; mixture should be steaming.
4. Pour cream mixture and coffee simultaneously into fat, heavy coffee mugs.
5. Garnish with a dollop of ice cream.

Makes 4 servings

Granny Glenn's Cider

1 ½ quarts apple cider
½ cup cinnamon candies (like Red Hots)
1 tsp whole cloves
cinnamon sticks

1. Pour cider and candies into a large saucepan.
2. Place cloves in a spice bag or small piece of cheesecloth, tie, and dump into cider.
3. Heat over medium and simmer about 15 to 20 minutes.
4. Serve hot in fun mugs (check out your thrift, second-hand, and antique stores).
5. Garnish with a cinnamon stick stirrer.

Makes 6 to 8 servings

St. Nick's Secret Brew

1 gallon apple cider
½ cup brown sugar
1 6-oz. can frozen lemonade
1 6-oz. can frozen orange juice
1 tblsp whole cloves
1 tblsp cinnamon
1 tblsp allspice
1 tblsp nutmeg
cinnamon sticks or small candy canes

1. In a large kettle mix cider, sugar, lemonade, and orange juice.

2. Tie cloves, cinnamon, allspice, and nutmeg in a spice bag or small square of cheesecloth, toss into brew, and simmer 20 minutes.

3. Serve hot with a cinnamon stick or candy cane stirrer.

Makes 30-36 servings

Buckin'Ham Palace's Hot Chocolate

2 ½ ounces unsweetened chocolate
½ cup cold water
¾ cup white sugar
dash of salt
½ tsp vanilla
¾ cup whipping cream, whipped stiff, divided
6 cups hot milk
ground cinnamon or nutmeg (optional)
grated chocolate

1. In the top of a double boiler heat water and chocolate together until melted.

2. Stir in sugar and salt and continue cooking until sugar dissolves and mixture thickens, about 5 minutes.

3. Cool and stir in vanilla. Reserve about 6 tablespoons whipped cream and fold remainder into chocolate mixture.

4. To each cup of hot milk stir in 1 1/2 tablespoons chocolate mixture and top with a dollop of reserved whipped cream.

5. Garnish with a sprinkle of cinnamon or nutmeg, if using, and grated chocolate.

Makes 6 servings

Matamoros España Chocolat

2 squares unsweetened chocolate
1 cup water
3 tblsps white sugar
dash of salt
3 cups milk
1 tsp. orange rind, grated
dash of almond extract
whipped cream

1. In the top of a double boiler add chocolate and water and place over low heat. Stir until well blended.

2. Add sugar and salt; place over direct heat, bring to boiling, and boil 4 minutes, stirring constantly.

3. Place back over boiling water; add milk gradually, stirring constantly.

4. Stir in orange rind, almond extract, and heat through.

5. Just before serving beat with hand mixer until light and foamy.

6. Pour into cups and garnish with whipped cream.

Makes 4 servings

Mount Saint Helens

3 cups brown sugar
3 cups white sugar
2 sticks (1 cup) butter, softened
1 quart vanilla ice cream, softened
1 tsp nutmeg
1 tsp cinnamon
rum flavoring
boiling water
cinnamon sticks

1. In your blender or with a hand mixer cream brown and white sugars with butter.
2. Add ice cream, nutmeg, and cinnamon; blend well.
3. To serve scoop 1 heaping tablespoon of the mixture into a mug, add 1 teaspoon rum flavoring, and fill with boiling water; stir.
4. Garnish with a cinnamon stick stirrer and serve.

Makes approximately 8 servings

The Bar is Open

Chapter 4

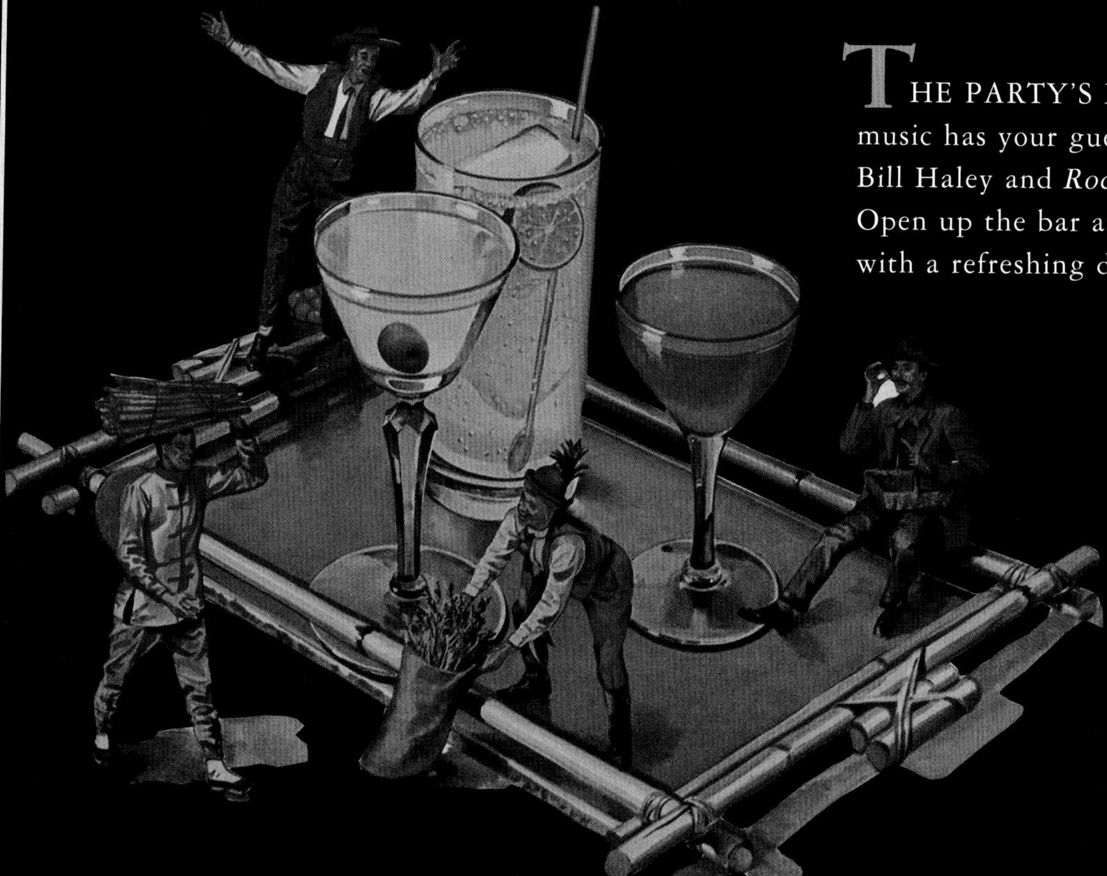

THE PARTY'S IN full swing. The music has your guests up and dancin' to Bill Haley and *Rock Around the Clock*. Open up the bar and delight your friends with a refreshing drink!

Punches with a Punch!

1732 Fish House Club Punch

The following recipe (or "receipt" as it was called in the really olden days) assumes about 1 1/2 drinks per guest. So, roughly figure out how much your guests will consume and multiply the following:

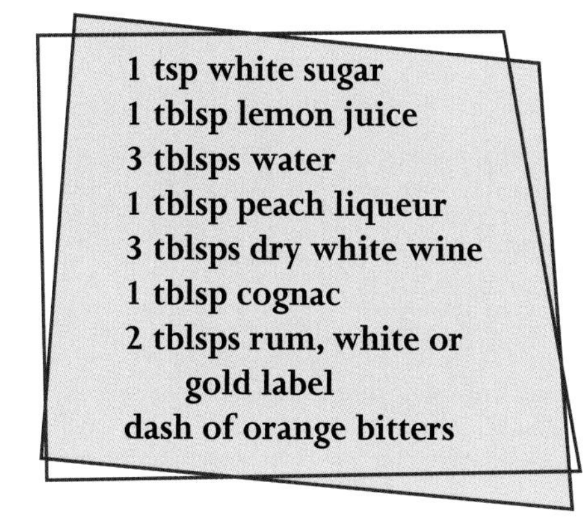
1 tsp white sugar
1 tblsp lemon juice
3 tblsps water
1 tblsp peach liqueur
3 tblsps dry white wine
1 tblsp cognac
2 tblsps rum, white or gold label
dash of orange bitters

1. Combine sugar, lemon juice, water, peach liqueur, white wine, cognac, rum, and orange bitters.
2. Let sit about 2 hours, stirring occasionally.
3. Serve in a nice punch bowl over a big chunk of ice or over ice in glasses. Mixture makes about 5 ounces.

Per person for 1 1/2 drinks

Swindler's Bay Punch

- 1 quart Burgundy wine
- 1 cup rum
- ⅓ cup brandy
- ⅓ cup Benedictine
- 1 quart soda water
- ½ cup crushed pineapple
- ¼ cup fresh lemon juice
- 1 cup strong hot Orange Pekoe tea
- sugar syrup to taste, about ¼ to ½ cup (see recipe on p. 88)
- 4 small oranges, sliced thin

1. In a large pitcher or bowl combine wine, rum, brandy, Benedictine, soda water, pineapple, lemon juice, tea, and sugar syrup.

2. Stir in orange slices. Pour over ice in your punch bowl.

Makes approximately 12 servings

Caribbean Pirate

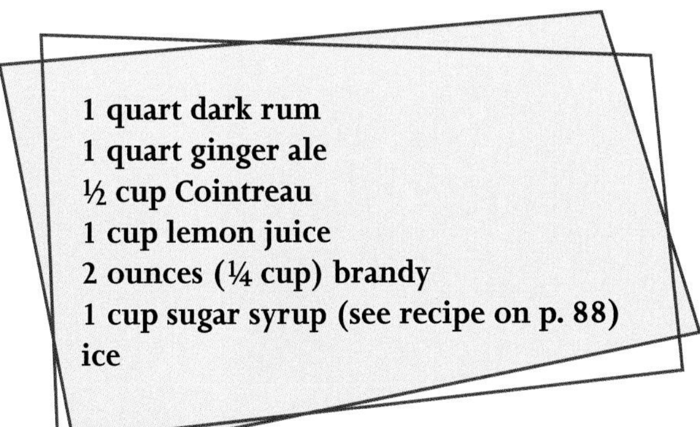

- 1 quart dark rum
- 1 quart ginger ale
- ½ cup Cointreau
- 1 cup lemon juice
- 2 ounces (¼ cup) brandy
- 1 cup sugar syrup (see recipe on p. 88)
- ice

1. In a large pitcher or bowl combine rum, ginger ale, Cointreau, lemon juice, brandy, and sugar syrup.

2. Pour over ice in your punch bowl.

Makes approximately 12 servings

Poolside Punch

¼ cup brandy
¼ cup curacao
grated rind from ½ orange (about 2 tsps)
grated rind from ½ lemon (about 2 tsps)
¼ cup sugar
1 quart sauterne
1 quart soda water or champagne
fresh strawberries, fresh mint leaves, or thin orange slices

1. In a medium glass bowl or pitcher combine brandy, curacao, orange and lemon rinds, and sugar. Let stand 2 hours.
2. Add sauterne. Strain and chill.
3. Just before serving add soda water or champagne.
4. Garnish with strawberries, mint, or orange slices.

Makes approximately 20 servings

Lord Byron's Claret Punch

1 quart claret
2 cups sugar syrup (see recipe on p. 88)
1 cup orange juice
1 cup lemon juice
1 quart water
1 quart soda water
½ orange, sliced thin
½ lemon, sliced thin
ice

1. In a large pitcher or bowl combine claret, sugar syrup, orange juice, lemon juice, water, and soda water.
2. Stir in orange and lemon slices.
3. Pour over ice in your punch bowl.

Makes approximately 36 servings

Tonga Tonga Punch Bowl

1 quart orange juice
1 ¼ cups lemon juice
½ cup lime juice
1 ¼ cups (10 oz.) orange curacao
1 quart light Puerto Rican rum
½ cup (4 oz.) grenadine
ice

1. In a large (gallon size) pitcher or jug mix orange juice, lemon juice, lime juice, curacao, rum, and grenadine.

2. Fill punch bowl with ice, pour punch mixture over ice, and stir thoroughly.

3. Add a few large chunks of ice. If you can get them, float a few gardenias or other tropical blossoms in the punch.

Makes 24-36 servings

Lighthouse Inn's Deck Party Punch

1 cup sugar syrup
(see recipe on p. 88)
1 quart fresh lemon juice
1 quart sparkling water
2 quarts Jamaican rum
1 quart brandy
10-pound block of ice

1. In a large punch bowl pour in sugar syrup, lemon juice, sparkling water, rum, and brandy. Stir together.

2. Add the block of ice and let punch stand 2 hours before serving. Stir occasionally.

Makes 36 servings

Polynesian Poolside Punch

8 oz. Triple Sec
8 oz. gin
3 oz. fresh lime juice
2 fifths chilled champagne
ice

1. Mix together Triple Sec, gin, lime juice, and champagne.

2. Place fist-size chunks of ice in a punch bowl and pour mixture over.

3. Let chill 30 minutes.

Makes 12-16 servings

Bangkok R&R Tea

This recipe came from Marine Corps friends returning from "rest and relaxation" in Bangkok, Thailand, during the Vietnam War.

Per serving:

1 oz. (2 tblsps) light rum
2 oz. (4 tblsps) hot strong black India-Ceylon tea
1 or 2 tsps white sugar (to taste)
lemon slices, cut very thin
nutmeg or whole cloves

1. In each heavy mug pour in rum, add tea and sugar, and fill with hot water. Stir.

2. Add a slice of lemon and dust with nutmeg.

3. If you prefer cloves, add 4 or 5 with the hot water.

Mint Juleps at the Greenbriar Inn

I would like to know how the Persian word *gulab* (*gul* for rose and *ab* for water) became julep — a famous Southern drink. The following is the equivalent for one of these delightful, refreshing drinks everyone carries around while track-side at the Kentucky Derby.

Per serving:

5 large fresh mint leaves (it's easy to grow in a shady spot in your yard or garden)
1 tsp sugar syrup (see p. 88)
3 to 4 tblsps bourbon (the very best bonded)
crushed ice
mint leaves

1. In a nice 8-ounce glass place mint leaves and crush with a knife handle or pestle. Add sugar syrup to taste.

2. Pour in bourbon and if possible allow to steep 15 minutes.

3. Fill glass with crushed ice and stir until glass is frosty.

4. Garnish with a mint leaf.

Sazerac Coffee House Cocktail

The origin for this drink dates back to 1870 in New Orleans. A few updates have been made, but essentially it's the same. The following is for each drink.

Per serving:

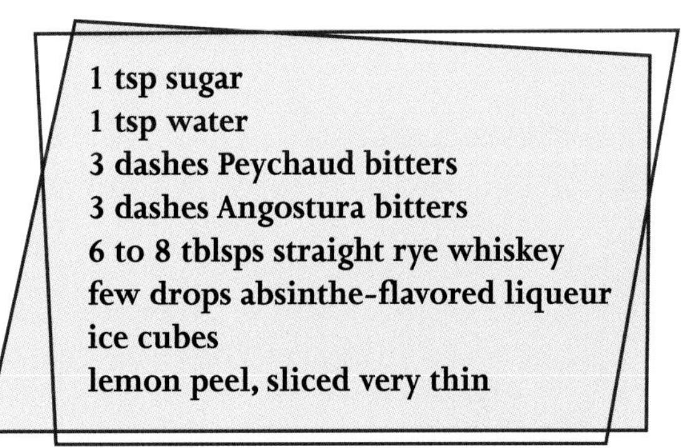

1 tsp sugar
1 tsp water
3 dashes Peychaud bitters
3 dashes Angostura bitters
6 to 8 tblsps straight rye whiskey
few drops absinthe-flavored liqueur
ice cubes
lemon peel, sliced very thin

1. Dissolve sugar in water and add bitters. Stir in rye, and if you can, let it mellow 2 hours in the refrigerator.

2. Pour liqueur into a wine or cocktail glass and roll glass gently to coat sides.

3. Add ice cubes and fill with rye mixture.

4. Garnish with lemon peel.

Kamehakameha Kahlua

2 ½ cups water, divided
2 cups white sugar
¼ cup instant coffee (must not be freeze dried and not the cheap kind)
1 fifth of vodka or brandy
1 vanilla bean

1. In a medium saucepan stir 2 cups water and sugar until sugar is dissolved; bring to a boil and boil 5 minutes.
2. Add coffee and 1/2 cup water. Let cool.
3. Add vodka or brandy and vanilla bean.
4. Let set at least 6 days before using.

Makes 2 quarts

Hill House Hammock

This drink is served at Hill House Inn with cucumber sandwiches. The sandwiches must be made by slicing unpeeled cukes very thin, sprinkling with salt and pepper, and using thin-sliced pumpernickel bread. You should be relaxing in a hammock when served.

Per serving:

1-½ jiggers Amer Picon
1-½ jiggers dry gin
½ jigger creme de cacao
shaved ice
strong black coffee, chilled
1 tblsp heavy cream

1. In an 8-ounce glass pour in Amer Picon, gin, and creme de cacao.

2. Fill glass with shaved ice. Pour in as much coffee as the glass will hold.

3. Float 1 tablespoon cream on top.

New Day Daiquiri

Per serving:

juice of ½ lime or ¼ lemon
1 tsp sugar
1 jigger (1 ½ oz.) light rum
1 banana or 6 fresh strawberries

1. Whirl juice of lime or lemon, sugar, and rum in blender with ice and either banana or strawberries.
2. Strain into cocktail glass.

Santa Margarita

Per serving:

slice of lemon
salt
1 jigger (1 ½ oz.) white Cuervo tequila
½ oz. Triple Sec
1 oz. fresh lemon or lime juice
cracked ice

1. Moisten rim of cocktail glass with slice of lemon, dip in salt.
2. Shake tequila, Triple Sec, and lemon or lime juice with cracked ice.
3. Strain into glass.

Hotel Hopkin's Desert Cooler

Per serving:

cracked ice
1 jigger (1 ½ oz.) Southern Comfort
8 oz. pineapple-grapefruit juice

1. Pack ice into tall glass, add Southern Comfort, and fill with juice.

Tree Trimmin' Party Drink

Per serving:

cinnamon stick
1 tsp sugar syrup (see recipe on p. 88)
1 thin slice lemon
1 jigger (1 ½ oz.) Jamaican rum
hot water
1 tsp real butter

1. Put cinnamon stick, sugar syrup, lemon slice, and rum in a nice hefty mug.
2. Fill mug with hot water and float butter on top. Stir.

Tower of London

Per serving:

1 jigger (1 ½ oz.) vodka
2 jiggers (3 oz.) tomato juice
½ jigger (¾ oz.) fresh lemon juice
dash of Worcestershire sauce
dash of salt
dash of coarsely ground black pepper
cracked ice
celery stick

1. Shake together until well chilled vodka, tomato juice, lemon juice, Worcestershire sauce, salt, and pepper.
2. Strain into a 6-oz. glass.
3. Garnish with celery stick.

Lightnin' Zapper

Per serving:

1 jigger (1 ½ oz.) brandy
½ jigger (¾ oz.) creme de menthe
cracked ice

1. Shake brandy and creme de menthe together well with ice.
2. Strain into a glass.

Alexander the Great

Per serving:

1 jigger (1 ½ oz.) Southern Comfort, gin, or brandy
3 tblsps fresh heavy cream
½ jigger (¾ oz.) creme de cacao
cracked ice

1. Shake Southern Comfort, gin, or brandy well with cream, creme de cacao, and cracked ice.
2. Strain into glass.

Biggie's Saint Loowee Cocktail

Per serving:

¾ oz. evaporated milk or cream
½ oz. white creme de cacao
½ oz. Cointreau
crushed ice

1. Shake well together evaporated milk or cream, creme de cacao, and Cointreau.
2. Strain into a cocktail glass.
3. Serve as an after-dinner drink.

Jackrabbit

Per serving:

750 ml bottle good bourbon
1 cup sugar
12 lemons cut in half
ice

1. In a glass pitcher, large jar, or crock pour in bourbon and sugar.
2. Squeeze lemons, add juice, and toss in leftover rinds.
3. Stir well. Cover and refrigerate overnight.
4. Remove lemon rinds.
5. Shake well with ice and strain into chilled cocktail glasses.

Tara O'Hara

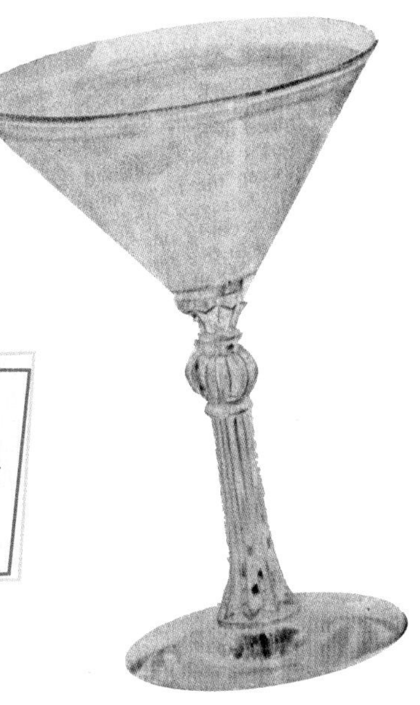

Per serving:

1 jigger (1 ½ oz.) Southern Comfort
1 jigger (1 ½ oz.) cranberry juice cocktail
2 tblsps fresh lime juice
cracked ice

1. Shake all ingredients with ice and strain into glass.

Jamaican Steel Drum

Per serving:

1 oz. orange juice
½ oz. lemon juice
¼ oz. grenadine
¼ oz. curacao
3 oz. light rum
3 oz. sparkling water
cracked ice
thin orange slices
fresh pineapple chunks
sprigs of fresh mint

1. In a cocktail shaker shake together orange juice, lemon juice, grenadine, curacao, rum, and sparkling water.

2. Pour into a 14-oz. chimney glass filled with ice and garnish with a thin slice of orange, a chunk of pineapple, and a sprig of mint.

Tiki Torcher

1. In your blender whirl together orange juice, lemon juice, rum, orgeat syrup, brandy, and shaved ice.

2. Blend well and pour into double old-fashioned glass with some cracked ice.

3. Top with a tropical flower if you have them available.

Per serving:

1 oz. orange juice
¾ oz. lemon juice
1 oz. light rum
¼ oz. orgeat syrup
½ oz. brandy
shaved ice
cracked ice

Orgeat Syrup

Orgeat syrup is a sweet syrup made from almonds, sugar and rose water/orange-flower water. It has a pronounced almond taste.

Orgeat syrup can be hard to find, but can be found in some stores that sell coffee syrups/flavorings. If you cannot find it, almond syrup is a good substitute.

Heartbroken Harry

Per serving:

shaved ice
3 tblsps lime juice
1 tblsp sugar syrup (see recipe on p. 88)
dash of orgeat syrup (see p. 122)
1 oz. light rum
dash of orange curacao
2 oz. dark rum
lime slice or sprig of mint

1. Fill a double old-fashioned glass with shaved ice; add ime juice, sugar syrup, orgeat syrup, light rum, orange curacao, and dark rum.

2. Cover with shaker and shake well.

3. Garnish with lime slice or sprig of mint.

Forbidden Fun

Per serving:

shaved ice
1-½ oz. unsweetened pineapple juice
½ oz. lemon juice
1 tsp sugar syrup (see recipe on p. 88)
1 oz. light rum
1 oz. vodka
fresh fruit slice
sprig of mint

1. In your blender add 1 scoop shaved ice; add pineapple juice, lemon juice, sugar syrup, rum, and vodka.
2. Blend 10 seconds.
3. Pour into a double old-fashioned glass.
4. Garnish with fruit slice or sprig of mint.

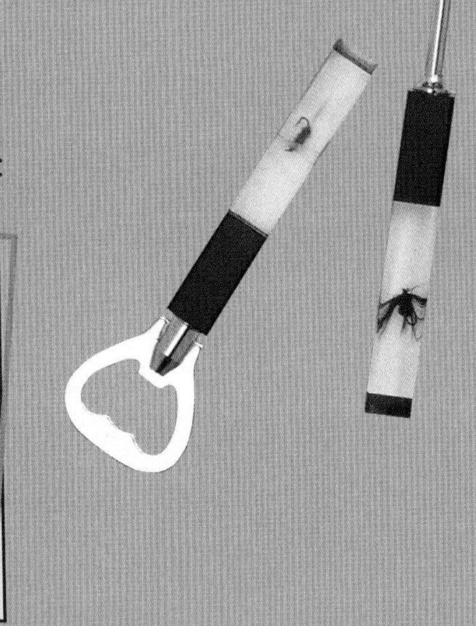

Foghorn

Per serving:

1 oz. orange juice
2 oz. lemon juice
½ oz. orgeat syrup (see p. 122)
2 oz. light rum
1 oz. brandy
½ oz. gin
sherry wine float
cracked ice

1. In a shaker add orange juice, lemon juice, orgeat syrup, rum, brandy, and gin.
2. Shake well and pour into a large (14 oz. or larger) glass.
3. Fill glass with ice and add sherry wine float.

Shark's Tooth

Per serving:

3 tblsps lime juice
½ oz. lemon juice
1 tsp sugar syrup
(see recipe on p. 88)
dash of grenadine
2-½ oz. gold rum
cracked ice
sparkling water
thin slice lime
fruit slices
sprigs of mint

1. In a glass pitcher stir lime juice, lemon juice, sugar syrup, grenadine, and rum.

2. Pour into large (10 oz. or larger) glass and fill with cracked ice; fill with sparkling water.

3. Garnish with lime or fruit slices and sprig of mint.

Singapore Slingshot

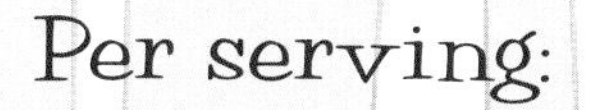

3 tblsps lime juice
dash of Angostura bitters
1 oz. Cherry Heering
2 oz. Old Tom gin
ginger beer
Benedictine float
cracked ice
thin lime slice
sprig of mint

1. Squeeze lime juice in a tall (10 oz. or larger) glass; add bitters, Cherry Heering, and gin.
2. Fill with ginger beer, stir, and add Benedictine float.
3. Garnish with lime slice and sprig of mint.

Index